THE
LONDON
THAMES
PATH

THE
LONDON
THAMES
PATH

A guide to the Thames Path
from Putney Bridge to the Barrier

Written & illustrated by
DAVID FATHERS

Also by David Fathers:
The Regent's Canal (2012)

In preparation:
London's Hidden Rivers

THE LONDON THAMES PATH
CONTENTS

Twenty bridges from Tower to Kew –
Wanted to know what the River knew,
For they were young and the Thames was old,
And this is the tale that the River told.

'The River's Tale' (1911), Rudyard Kipling

Contents map	6
Using this book	8
Introduction	9
The North Shore: A prelude	11
Fulham	12
Chelsea Harbour	14
Cheyne Walk	16
Chelsea Embankment	18
Pimlico	20
Millbank	22
Westminster	24
Westminster Abbey	26
Victoria Embankment	28
Sir Joseph Bazalgette	30
Victoria Embankment Gardens	32
Temple	34
St Paul's	36
Walbrook	38
Sir Christopher Wren	40
Pool of London	42
Tower of London	44
St Katherine Docks	46
Wapping	48
A Word on the Water	50
Limehouse	52
Canary Wharf	54
Island Gardens	56
Cubitt Town	58
Blackwall	60
Thames Barrier	62
The South Shore: A prelude	65
Putney	66
Battersea Reach	68
Battersea Park	70
Nine Elms	72
Vauxhall	74
Albert Embankment	76
Lambeth Palace	78
The Watermen	80
London Eye	82
South Bank	84
National Theatre	86
The Frost Fairs	88
Bankside	90
Southwark Cathedral	92
Old London Bridge	94
City Hall	96
The Shard	98
Bermondsey	100
Death and the Thames	102
Rotherhithe	104
Surrey Commercial Docks	106
Deptford	108
Greenwich	110
Greenwich Peninsula	112
Bugsby's Reach	114
The London Thames Crossings	116
The Thames Estuary	118
Acknowledgements, Bibliography	120
Index	123

THE LONDON THAMES PATH
CONTENTS

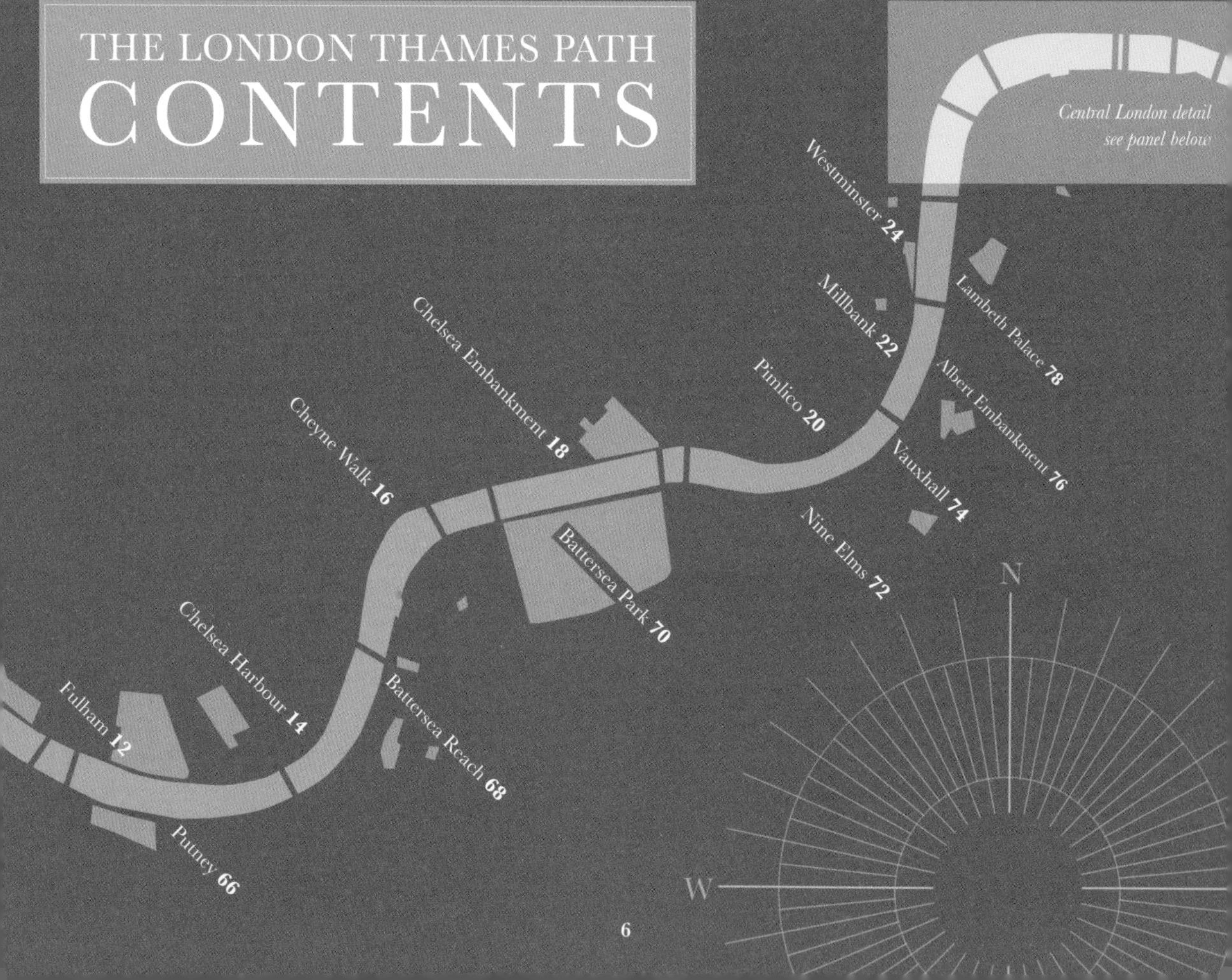

Central London detail
see panel below

Westminster **24**

Millbank **22**

Lambeth Palace **78**

Pimlico **20**

Albert Embankment **76**

Chelsea Embankment **18**

Vauxhall **74**

Cheyne Walk **16**

Nine Elms **72**

Battersea Park **70**

Chelsea Harbour **14**

Battersea Reach **68**

Fulham **12**

Putney **66**

N

W

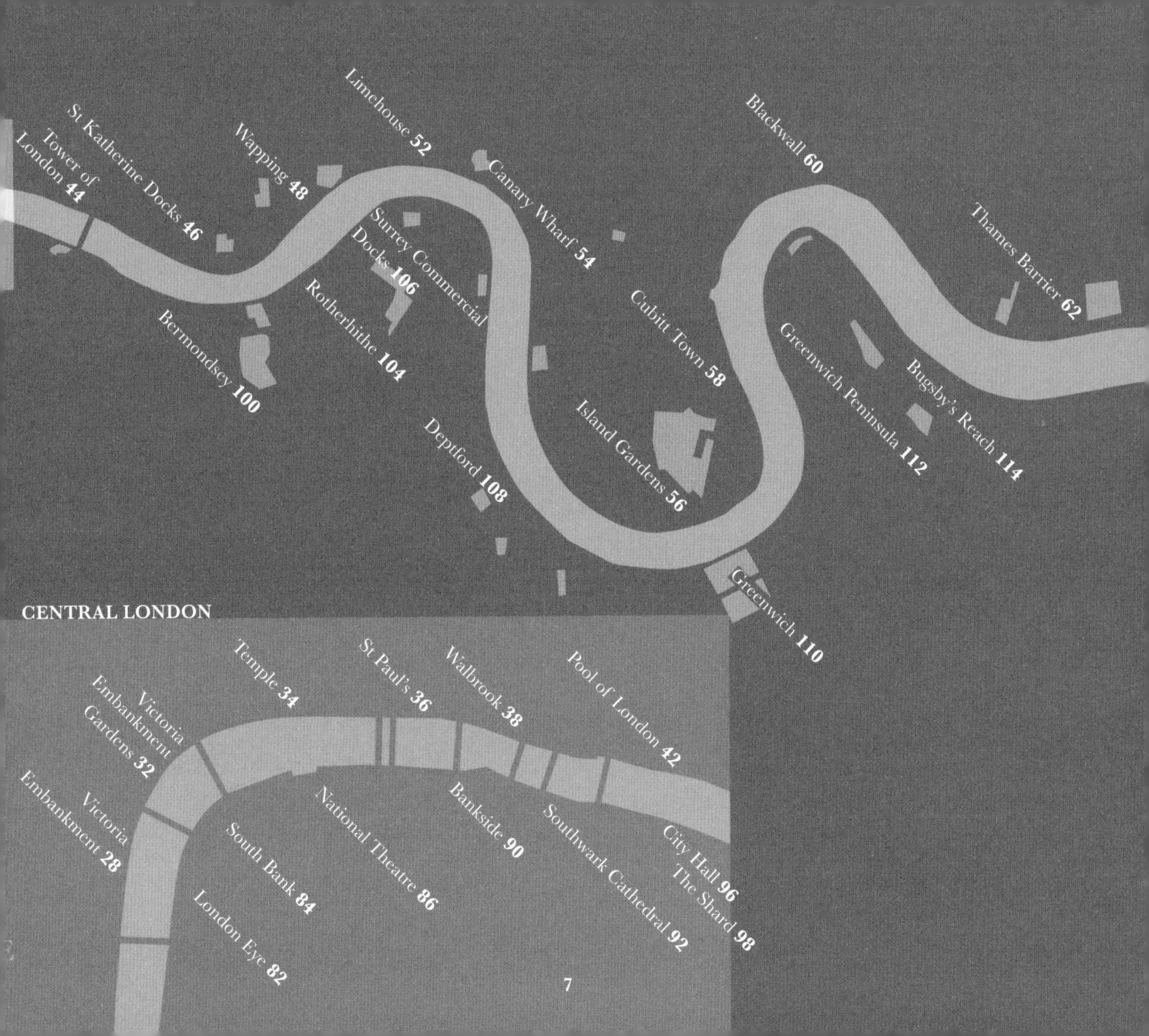

Tower of
London **44**

St Katherine Docks **46**

Wapping **48**

Limehouse **52**

Canary Wharf **54**

Blackwall **60**

Thames Barrier **62**

Surrey Commercial
Docks **106**

Cubitt Town **58**

Greenwich Peninsula **112**

Bugsby's Reach **114**

Bermondsey **100**

Rotherhithe **104**

Island Gardens **56**

Deptford **108**

Greenwich **110**

CENTRAL LONDON

Temple **34**

St Paul's **36**

Walbrook **38**

Pool of London **42**

Victoria
Embankment
Gardens **32**

Victoria
Embankment **28**

South Bank **84**

National Theatre **86**

Bankside **90**

Southwark Cathedral **92**

City Hall **96**

The Shard **98**

London Eye **82**

7

Using this book

There are 65km (40 miles) of walks detailed in this book, but they are not seriously intended to be walked in one go. Circular walks can be planned by adding together the distances marked on each section, plus approximately 300m per bridge. East of Tower Bridge there are no further bridge crossings, though there is a rail tunnel between Wapping and Rotherhithe, a foot tunnel at Greenwich and a ferry between Hilton Docklands and Canary Wharf.

Short sections of the Thames Path are occasionally closed due to building or repair work (or even floods). Signs are normally displayed to show the detours.

The Thames Path is shown throughout by a red dotted line and with steps where access is required up or down to and from bridges. The nearest Underground, DLR and railway stations are also featured along with Thames Clipper piers. The Thames path is often indicated with signs such as the one below.

• • •   *Thames Path*   *Underground station*

 ⌐   *Steps*   *DLR station*

 ⇥   *National Rail station*   *Thames Clipper pier*

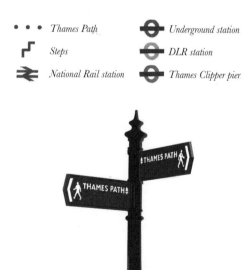

INTRODUCTION

To walk the London Thames Path is to explore a vital artery of one of the greatest cities on earth. For over 2,000 years the river has shaped London's development, and more recently Londoners have shaped the river itself. The capital's entire existence was founded upon the Thames, which was the conduit of power and trade, finance and security, but it also brought floods, wars, plagues and disasters.

CONTROL

Power has always resided beside the water's edge in London. The Romans built their first fortification around what is now known as Ludgate Hill, where St Paul's Cathedral now stands. William the Conqueror chose to site his castle, the Tower of London, just to the east of the City, upon an existing Roman fort. Numerous English kings and queens have located their palaces and castles beside the Thames, at Greenwich and Whitehall, Windsor and Hampton. These were places of security, safely accessible by water. Politicians and clergy also desired proximity to the river's edge at Westminster and Lambeth. In the past hundred years or more, local London politicos have sited their County and City Halls along the south bank.

TRADE

For millennia, goods have been carried along the Thames, either between the two shores or by vessels trading beyond London. The river, though tidal, was the most convenient form of transporting of goods and people. Access to the water enabled so many industries to develop – to get raw materials in and finished goods out. By the early twentieth century, London was the largest city on earth, and a hub of industry the likes of which had not been seen. From biscuits to paint, from pianos to ships . . . just about everything and anything was being manufactured in the metropolis. William Blake's 'dark Satanic Mills' was a reference to the belching factory chimneys of the south bank. The riverbanks were crammed with warehouses, cranes and shipping.

As London and the British Empire grew, the demands for greater port access likewise increased. Shipping, tied up in the middle of the Thames, had to wait days, sometimes weeks, to either dock or be unloaded by lightermen in their smaller vessels. Larger and larger docks were created further downstream in the early 1800s, first at St Katherine's, then Wapping and Rotherhithe, and later at the Isle of Dogs and North Woolwich. The river became a superhighway of ships and merchant vessels. A sizeable area of East London had been excavated and filled with water (*see map: overleaf*). However, the demands of trade led, by the 1970s, to containerisation and deepwater ships. London, a victim of its own success, could no longer compete, and the river traffic drifted away to ports further downstream, such as Tilbury and Harwich.

It is difficult now to imagine the amount of shipping that used to be tied up in the river waiting to be unloaded and loaded. Traffic on the Thames today is a mere ripple by comparison. The warehouses have been converted into fine loft appartments, the offices and the cranes turned to scrap, and many of the inland ports have been filled in and built upon. On the Isle of Dogs, in the 1980s, a whole new commercial venture was created on the site of the docks. Canary Wharf replaced physical trading with financial transaction.

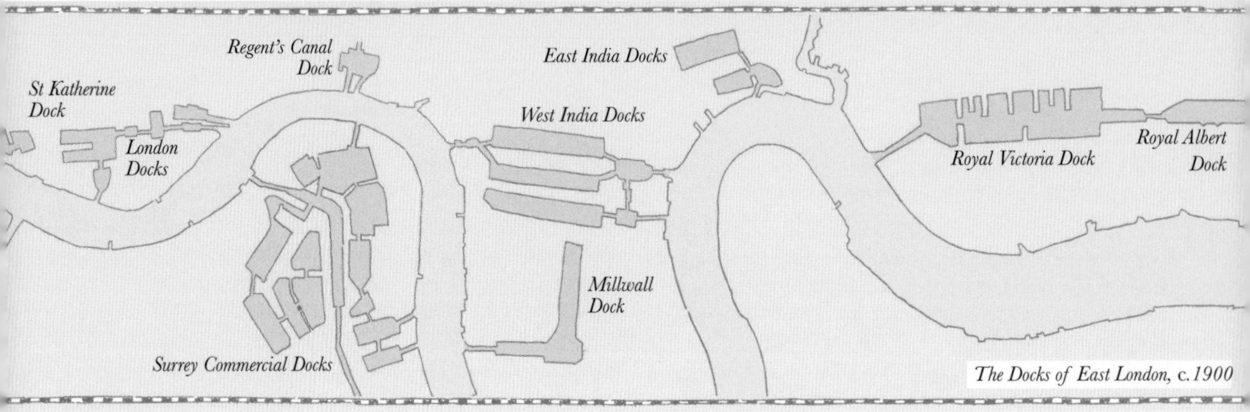

The Docks of East London, c.*1900*

THE GREAT STINK

Prior to the nineteenth century, the Thames in London was, in places, three times the width we see today. Much of the land, especially to the south, consisted of marshland and tidal flood plains. Londoners had made some piecemeal progress in creating embankments to prevent erosion and create accessible moorings.

By 1861, the population of Greater London had trebled to over 3 million in just sixty years. The sewage infrastructure was unable to cope and nearly all human ordure and industrial waste still ended up in the Thames. Drinking water was still being taken from the river and the risk of epidemics increased. The 'Great Stink' from the Thames forced Parliament to relocate in 1858, shortly after the Metropolitan Board of Works was established to create an integrated sewage system with processing plants, and to embank and narrow the river, thus increasing the speed of tidal flow to flush away foul waters.

THE FALL AND RISE

In the 150 years prior to 1900, twelve bridges were built over the river in London. This drastically reduced the need for water taxis and lightermen carrying people and goods from shore to shore. Containerised shipping took most of the maritime trade away from London. At around the same time heavy industry in the capital went into decline. London has turned to other trades and commercial activities, but not ones that depend upon the Thames.

Today the river is enjoying a new lease of life. It is cleaner now than it has been for hundreds of years. Fish are regularly caught along the banks of the Thames and seals and dolphins are occasionally sighted. In a bid to improve their green credentials, many companies are increasingly using the Thames to move materials in and refuse out by barge. Tourist boats and a regular 'waterbus' service ply along the water. Even though the English monarchs have abandoned their London riverside palaces, those who can afford and desire to live by the Thames, can now do so. Several seats of power still cling to the river, though now through a sense of tradition.

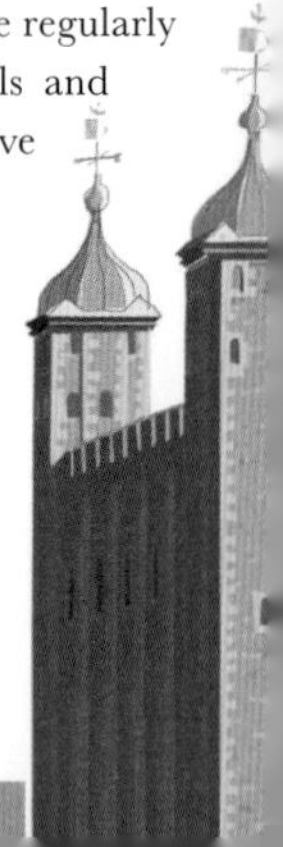

THE NORTH SHORE:
A prelude

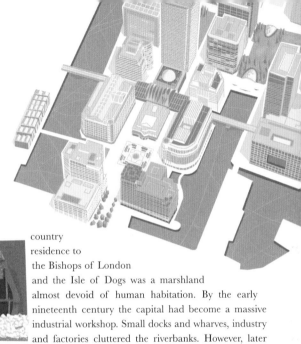

The walk along the north shore of the London Thames described in this book covers a distance of just over 33km (20 miles). Whilst a large percentage follows the bank of the river, occasionally the route detours away from the Thames. Ancient property rights have prevented the creation of riverside walks.

Officially, the Thames Path stops at the Greenwich Foot Tunnel. However, I have taken a route on to the Thames Barrier in order to explore some splendid Thamesside and Dockland features. On this northern shore, if you walk from west to east, through Fulham and Chelsea to the renovated Docklands and finally the Thames Barrier, you will pass through Westminster, the very heart of power, where Government, Monarchy and Church reside. Step further on to Temple and the City of London and you are treading upon strata of maritime trade and business, culture and bloodshed that span some 2,000 years.

Since the Romans first encamped around the River Walbrook, the docks to the east of the City have been inextricably linked with the heart of finance and commerce. This interdependence continued until about the 1970s. Whilst the docks have declined from a leading global position, the City has continued to thrive and occupy new spaces vacated by the warehouses and docks on the Isle of Dogs.

In a space of 200 years, so much has changed: Fulham was still market gardens and country residence to the Bishops of London and the Isle of Dogs was a marshland almost devoid of human habitation. By the early nineteenth century the capital had become a massive industrial workshop. Small docks and wharves, industry and factories cluttered the riverbanks. However, later that century almost all these vestiges were swept away when the river was narrowed and embanked to channel sewage away from the Thames. By Bow Creek, as it enters the Thames, there was once a huge shipbuilding yard, yet to walk over it today, hardly a rivet remains.

Clockwise from left: The Tower of London, Map of the Docks, the Walbrook sluice gate, Canary Wharf and the Thames Barrier.

Fulham Palace

This is one of the least known of all London's palaces, yet it is a gem of a place, close to the river. A newly restored walled garden, tree-lined walks and a splendid Tudor hall are located within this 11 hectare site. Bishops have resided here since about AD 700, and from Tudor times the palace has served as country retreat for the Bishops of London. The river gave them direct access to the seats of power at Westminster and Hampton Court. Bishop Stopford was the last bishop to reside here, moving out in 1973. The buildings, café and public gardens are now run by the local council. Access to most areas is free of charge.

Fulham Palace

Right: Entrance to the walled garden

Café

Walled garden

◁Thames Path to Hammersmith

All Saints Church

This church was constructed in 1440 on a previous site of worship. It is largely constructed of Kentish ragstone, brought up by boat. The tower is the only remaining original feature, the rest of the church being rebuilt in the early 1880s. At least ten Bishops of London are buried in the churchyard. All Saints church was featured in the 1976 version of *The Omen*. Father Brennan (played by Patrick Troughton) was impaled by a falling lightning rod.

The Boat Race

Putney Bridge is the starting point of the annual rowing race between the university boat clubs of Oxford and Cambridge. The first race was held in 1829 and has continued uninterrupted since 1856 (except during the two World Wars). Over a quarter of a million people line the banks of the Thames to watch the race, plus millions on TV, on either the last Saturday of March or the first Saturday of April. The finish line is 6.8km upstream at Mortlake. They race on an incoming flood tide.

Putney Bridge Approach

Putney Railway Bridge

First opened to rail traffic in 1889 and constructed of Portland stone and steel, it now carries the Wimbledon branch of the District line.

Putney Bridge Underground

Putney Railway Bridge

Putney Bridge

ON THE OTHER BANK
St Mary's page 66

12

FULHAM

Fulham Palace – Broomhouse Lane

2,200m In the early nineteenth century, Fulham was still rural with market gardens supplying fresh produce to the growing London population. It is now a largely affluent residential area.

Hurlingham Club

In the eighteenth century, Fulham was considered a rural area. Many of the wealthy from London built country retreats here. In 1760, Dr William Cadogan, an advocate and writer on radical child care, had a house built for himself and his family. One hundred years later, the building, Hurlingham House, became a club and home to pigeon shooting. In 1874 polo was introduced and the club became renowned for the sport and created the governing body, known as Hurlingham Polo Association. However, polo is no longer played here. Hurlingham Club is now a private club offering tennis, croquet and swimming. The grounds and the riverfront are inaccessible to non-members.

The Elizabethan Schools

In 1855 this piece of Gothic Revival architecture *(above)* was built as a 'ragged' school and almshouse. It is currently being converted into residential apartments.

Hurlingham Road

Napier Avenue

Ranelagh Gardens

A defensive Second World War pillbox (above) remains by the Underground line and is visible from Ranelagh Gardens.

Broomhouse Lane

Carnwath Road

CHELSEA HARBOUR

Carnwath Road – Lots Road 3,000m

In the late 1880s, this land, running down to the Thames at Wandsworth Bridge, was still largely occupied by market gardens. Today it is a very unprepossessing area, comprising modern warehouses and retail outlets. Beyond the bridge, however, as the path turns north, the imposing Chelsea Harbour comes into view.

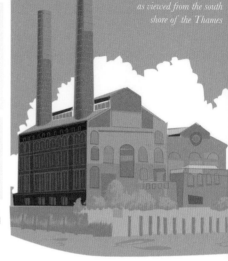

Lots Road Power Station, as viewed from the south shore of the Thames

The austere Wandsworth Bridge

Carnwath Road

△ *River Wandle*

Wandsworth Bridge Road

Sainsbury's

ON THE OTHER BANK
Solid Waste Transfer Depot and
River Wandle page 67

Imperial Wharf

These new and anonymous blocks of apartments *(right)*, set back and surrounded by well manicured gardens, announce to the eastbound walker and cyclist that this is the beginning of extensive riverside developments along the Thames. Between here and the Isle of Dogs, hardly a scrap of land is sacred or untouchable. The site was formerly a biscuit works and the Imperial Timber wharf.

Wandsworth Bridge

When the first Wandsworth Bridge opened in 1873, it was riddled with structural problems. In 1897 the speed of crossing traffic had to be restricted to 10 mph and it was reduced virtually to the status of a footbridge. Demands for its replacement

Lots Road Power Station

This former electricity generating station stands on what was once the Cremorne Pleasure Gardens *(see page 16)*. It opened in 1905 to supply power to the Brompton and Piccadilly Circus Railway (now the Piccadilly line). Coal was supplied to the generating station by barges coming up the Thames and into what was then known as Counter's Creek (now Chelsea Creek). In the 1960s the number of chimneys on the power station was reduced from four to two. From a distance it must have resembled Battersea power station *(see page 72)*. It was decommissioned in 2002 and is now being converted into retail and residential facilities.

Above: Site of The Imperial Gas Works.

Chelsea Harbour

This modern, eclectic and expensive development *(below right)* of residential apartments, offices, shops and a hotel encircles a marina that was once the railway dock for the Kensington Canal (now Chelsea Creek). Chelsea Harbour was built between 1986 and 1989 and despite its name, is actually located in Fulham. The Belvedere Tower is twenty-one storeys/76m high and is a landmark feature. The apex is topped with a golden tide ball that rises and falls with the tidal river.

Imperial Wharf Overground

Chelsea Harbour Dr.

Lots Road

Lots Road Power Station

Chelsea Creek

Imperial Wharf

Chelsea Creek

This spur is all that remains of the 3.2km Kensington Canal, which was built in 1828 by dredging and widening Counter's Creek. One of its functions was to provide easy access for coal barges to the Imperial Gas Works, some of the gas holders of which are still visible.

Chelsea Harbour Pier

Imperial Wharf Marina

Battersea Railway Bridge

were not fully realised until 1940. Due to wartime financial restraints, the bridge has a very utilitarian appearance *(opposite page)*.

ON THE OTHER BANK
St Mary's Church page 69

15

CHEYNE WALK

Lots Road – Cheyne Walk 1,240m

When Chelsea was a village beyond London, Cheyne Walk was a quiet riverside walkway lined with fine houses and trees overlooking the Thames. In 1874, the Chelsea Embankment was created, narrowing the river at this point; the carriageway was widened and a major sewer laid below. The road is now extremely busy at times but it does not mask the serenity of the architecture just beyond.

Crosby Hall

This building was originally located in Bishopsgate in the City of London and was known in the fifteenth century as one of the tallest buildings in the country. It was built by the wool merchant John Crosby and was once home to Sir Thomas More. In 1908 it was threatened with demolition and was remarkably moved, brick by brick, to its current location in Chelsea. Now owned by Christopher Moran, the Chairman of Co-operation Ireland, it is currently closed to the public and undergoing a multi-million-pound restoration.

Cremorne Gardens

This tiny patch of grass *(lower left corner)* by the river is all that remains of what was the last of the great London 'pleasure gardens'. It opened in 1845 and gave the London populace the opportunity to indulge in theatre, dancing, bowls, music and banqueting. For a while, in 1848, it featured the world's first 'steam powered aeroplane'. The artist James McNeill Whistler, a local inhabitant, created several paintings of the gardens. By the 1860s it had developed a reputation for promiscuity and it was closed down in 1877, following a campaign by various local churches. Much of the grounds, stretching as far as King's Road, were sold off for housing and manufacturing enterprises.

Cremorne Pleasure Gardens

*Right: Crosby Hall.
Below: Statue of
the artist J.M.
Whistler.*

Beaufort Street

Cheyne Walk

Chelsea Embankmer

Battersea Bridge

In 1771, a wooden bridge consisting of nineteen spans (or piers) crossed the river at a point that had once been a horse ferry crossing. It featured in several paintings by local artists, including J.M.W. Turner and James McNeill Whistler. By the 1880s, the bridge was reduced to a footbridge. The current bridge *(right)*, designed by Sir Joseph Bazalgette, consists of five cast-iron arches on granite piers and was opened in 1890. At 12m wide it is one of the narrowest crossings in London.

Battersea Bridge

Lots Road

Cremorne
Gardens

Chelsea Old Church (All Saints)

This church, dating from 1157, with its original interior, is built of brick, as it was badly damaged during the Blitz in the Second World War. A statue of a stern, gold-faced Sir Thomas More sits outside the church. More, Lord Chancellor to Henry VIII and author of *Utopia*, lived near by and had a private chapel built within the church. More was later executed for his beliefs in Papal supremacy over the English throne.

Right: A memorial to mark the opening of the Chelsea Embankment in 1874, located outside the Chelsea Old Church.

Chelsea Manor

Located at the site of 19–26 Cheyne Walk, Chelsea Manor was once a country home to Henry VIII and a number of his wives. The building was demolished after the death of it last owner, Sir Hans Sloane, in 1753. Sloane is buried in a splendid tomb within the grounds of Chelsea Old Church.

Blue Plaque Heaven

Cheyne Walk has been an address for many writers, artists and engineers of the past few hundred years. This short street is awash with blue plaques.

House no.:

4	George Eliot *Novelist*
16	Dante Gabriel Rossetti *Painter*
24	Thomas Carlyle *Philosopher*
93	Elizabeth Gaskell *Novelist*
96	J.M.Whistler *Painter*
98	Isambard Kingdom Brunel and Sir Marc Isambard Brunel *Civil engineers*
104	Hilaire Belloc *Poet and historian* Walter Greaves *Artist*
108	John Tweed *Sculptor*
109	Philip Wilson Steer *Painter*
120	Sylvia Pankhurst *Women's rights campaigner*

Henry James, T.S. Eliot, Ian Fleming all lived at Carlyle Mansion on Cheyne Walk. It became known as 'Writers' Block'.

DANTE GABRIEL ROSSETTI 1828 – 1882 AND ALGERNON CHARL SWINBURN 1837 – 1909 lived here

LONDON COUNTY C

Below: The site of Chelsea Manor.

Oakley Street

Cheyne Walk

ON THE OTHER BANK
Albion Riverside page 69

Thomas More

Cheyne Walk

Chelsea Embankment

Albert Bridge

Cadogan Pier

CHELSEA EMBANKMENT
Cheyne Walk – Chelsea Bridge Road 1,000m

The eastern end of the Chelsea Embankment is a very verdant section of the urban Thames. Several old parks and gardens have survived the onslaught of metropolitan expansion, including the Royal Hospital and the Chelsea Physic Gardens. Battersea Park can be viewed across the river. The Chelsea Embankment is the straightest section of the Thames in London.

Chelsea Physic Garden

This garden was created in 1673 by the Worshipful Society of Apothecaries to study the medicinal properties of plants. The land on which it stood was purchased by Sir Hans Sloane and leased back to the Society in perpetuity for £5 a year. The location *(below)*, so close to the river, gives the garden a micro-climate that enables more exotic plants to survive. The garden is open to the public.

Royal Hospital Chelsea

The hospital was founded by Charles II in 1682 to provide housing for retired and injured army veterans. The building today *(right)* is still occupied by retired soldiers, better known today as Chelsea Pensioners, easily identified by their scarlet tunics. The grand Baroque red-brick structure was designed by Sir Christopher Wren and was one of his first secular commissions. It is built on three sides around the Figure Court, open to the south grounds and the river beyond. The chapel, also by Wren, contains a splendid altar fresco of the Resurrection by Sebastiano Ricci. In the Great Hall, the Duke of Wellington lay in state in 1852. A vivid, gilded statue of Charles II dressed as a Roman emperor stands in the middle of the central Figure Court. Much of the Hospital and grounds are open to the public.

Right: A Chelsea Pensioner and the main Hospital portico.
Left: The Chelsea Physic Garden.

Royal Hospital Road

Chelsea Embankment

ON THE OTHER BANK
Battersea Park
page 71

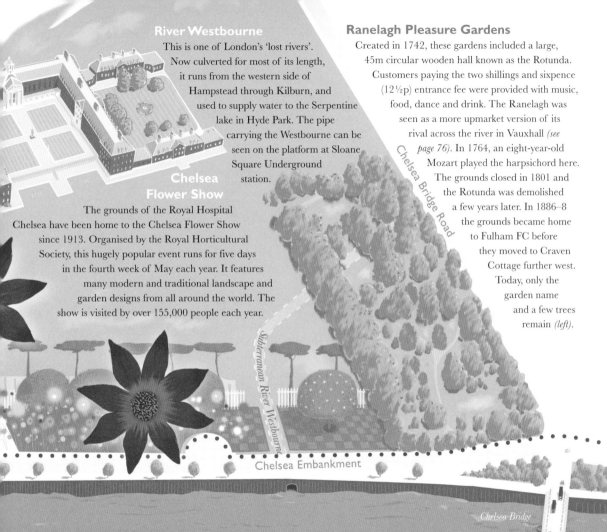

River Westbourne

This is one of London's 'lost rivers'. Now culverted for most of its length, it runs from the western side of Hampstead through Kilburn, and used to supply water to the Serpentine lake in Hyde Park. The pipe carrying the Westbourne can be seen on the platform at Sloane Square Underground station.

Chelsea Flower Show

The grounds of the Royal Hospital Chelsea have been home to the Chelsea Flower Show since 1913. Organised by the Royal Horticultural Society, this hugely popular event runs for five days in the fourth week of May each year. It features many modern and traditional landscape and garden designs from all around the world. The show is visited by over 155,000 people each year.

Ranelagh Pleasure Gardens

Created in 1742, these gardens included a large, 45m circular wooden hall known as the Rotunda. Customers paying the two shillings and sixpence (12½p) entrance fee were provided with music, food, dance and drink. The Ranelagh was seen as a more upmarket version of its rival across the river in Vauxhall *(see page 76)*. In 1764, an eight-year-old Mozart played the harpsichord here. The grounds closed in 1801 and the Rotunda was demolished a few years later. In 1886–8 the grounds became home to Fulham FC before they moved to Craven Cottage further west. Today, only the garden name and a few trees remain *(left)*.

Chelsea Bridge Road

Subterranean River Westbourne

Chelsea Embankment

Chelsea Bridge

Grosvenor Canal

This small tidal inlet was originally an access point for the Chelsea Waterworks Company to pump water from the Thames and supply it as drinking water to parts of London. In the 1820s, the inlet was extended further northwards as a canal with locks, to allow barges to carry building materials and coal for the growing estates around Belgravia and Pimlico. It was known as the Grosvenor Canal. By the 1850s, the water company had gone and canal use declined. The canal basin was filled in to make way for Victoria station, which opened in 1860. During the twentieth century, this already short canal was truncated further and is now just an ornamental water feature for the newly built office blocks surrounding it.

The Western Pumping Station

This Italianate building *(below left)* was opened in 1875 to house a sewage pumping station. Four steam, now electric, engines raised raw sewage up into the main Thames Embankment pipe and on to the Beckton treatment works. It forms part of Sir Joseph Bazalgette's grand Victorian sewerage network for London.

Far left: Lock entrance to the Thames. Above: Chelsea Bridge.

Chelsea Bridge

The building of Battersea Park in the 1850s resulted in the demand for a new bridge to allow easier access to the park from the north shore. Both the park and the bridge (designed by Thomas Page) were opened by Queen Victoria on the same day in 1858. By the 1930s, the bridge had become too small for the demands of the twentieth century. It was demolished and a more utilitarian successor opened in 1937 *(above)*.

Grosvenor Railway Bridge

This was the first railway bridge to span the Thames in London. It opened in 1860 to link Victoria station with the south coast. The bridge has been widened twice – in 1866 and 1907 – and the number of tracks increased to ten. The bridge took its name from the Grosvenor Canal over which it was built. In the 1960s the entire structure was modernised.

Chelsea Bdge Rd

Chelsea Bridge

Grosvenor Road

PIMLICO

Chelsea Bridge Road – St George's Square 1,176m

Pimlico is an area of riverside dwelling created largely by the builder Thomas Cubitt in the second quarter of the nineteenth century. It was raised out of the marshland from the spoils dug from St Katherine Docks. Despite the stuccoed terraces, the area was still very industrialised, with gas works to the east and brewery and pumping station and canal to the west.

Dolphin Square

This huge brick-built edifice *(below)* was constructed in 1937 and was at the time the largest block of flats in Europe. Standing over Cubitt's building yard, it has 1,250 apartments over 3.2 hectares. The hot water supply used to come from Battersea Power Station across the river. The facilities within this secure residence include a swimming pool, a gym, and tennis and croquet courts. Given its proximity to Westminster, it is second home to numerous Members of Parliament and senior civil servants.

William Huskisson

Huskisson (1770–1830) was a politician, best known as the first victim of rail travel. He was struck by Stephenson's steam engine *Rocket* in 1830. The marble statue *(far right)*, commissioned by his wife, was originally located in Liverpool before being moved to Pimlico Gardens.

St George's Square

This is the only residential square that opens onto the Thames. This long thin 'square' *(left)* was part of Thomas Cubitt's grand plan for Pimlico to provide elegant stuccoed terraces for the growing middle classes of London in the 1840s. At number 26, Bram Stoker, author of *Dracula*, died in 1912. Pimlico Gardens form the southern end of St George's Square.

Grosvenor Road

Westminster Boating Base

ON THE OTHER BANK
Battersea Power Station page 72

21

MILLBANK

St George's Square – Lambeth Bridge 1,460m

Beyond the stuccoed terraces of Pimlico and on to Millbank, Tate Britain's suggestion of culture and refinement hides a dark past. On this site once stood the notorious Millbank Penitentiary. Many of the prisoners being held here were about to be transported to Australia. This was the last time their feet would touch British soil.

River Tyburn

The source of the now-subterranean River Tyburn is in Hampstead, north London. As it flows south it travels over the Regent's Canal in an iron conduit, through an antiques shop basement and under the front of Buckingham Palace. Until the late 1960s, the final few hundred metres of the river were still exposed. A rebuilt sluicegate keeper's house still exists by the River Thames.

Millbank Penitentiary

This was the UK's first 'modern' prison. From above it appeared as a six-pointed star or snowflake *(see plan right)*, with the control hub at the centre of the institution. The design was partially influenced by the 'panopticon' prison layout of the social theorist Jeremy Bentham. The Millbank Penitentiary, opened in 1816, and would eventually hold over 850 prisoners. It became a clearing-house for those sentenced to be transported to Australia. The convicted would be moved downstream on small vessels to the transportation ships moored off Woolwich. The prison closed in 1890 and the land is now covered by Tate Britain and Chelsea College of Art.

Pimlico Underground

Subterranean River Tyburn

A small section of the ditch (right) that surrounded the prison has survived, and is still visible on the bend of Cureton Street.

Penitentiary

Gate

Cureton St

Vauxhall Bridge Road

John Islip St

Bessborough Gardens

Grosvenor Road

alternative footpath

Vauxhall Bridge

Looking Pieces by Henry Moore in Riverside Walk Gardens

Millbank Estate

Behind Tate Britain stands a series of workers' housing blocks built in the Arts and Crafts style. They were completed in 1902. Appropriately, given the location, each block is named after a British artist.

Left: A typical doorway on the Millbank Estate. Right: Clore Gallery entrance. Below: Millbank Tower. Below right: Thames House.

Tate Britain

The gallery was created in 1897 by Sir Henry Tate, a manufacturer and sugar refiner. Tate used his profits to develop a gallery on the site of the old penitentiary to house his collection of British art. The architect Sidney R.J. Smith created a large porticoed frontage facing the Thames. The Tate Gallery, as it was originally known, grew in size as new collections were acquired from both the UK and overseas. Additional galleries have been added over the years, including the Postmodernist Clore Gallery (1987), designed by Sir James Stirling and Wilford Associates to house the J.M.W. Turner collection. By the early 1990s, the Trustees of the Tate decided to split the ever-expanding London-based collection into several parts and to create a new gallery further downstream at Bankside to be known as Tate Modern *(see page 90)*. The Millbank gallery, Tate Britain, now displays exclusively British art.

Millbank Tower

This thirty-two-storey tower opened in 1963 and at 118m high it briefly held the record for the tallest building in the UK. The tower, with its convex and concave sides, was designed by Ronald Ward & Partners and was inspired by the works of Mies van der Rohe, a pioneer of Modernist architecture. Originally built for the Vickers-Armstrong Group, it has become best known more recently as the headquarters of the Labour Party between 1995 and 2000. It is now a Grade II listed building.

Lambeth Bridge

Millbank

Millbank Millennium Pier

ON THE OTHER BANK
MI6 HQ page 75

Thames House

This stone-clad Neoclassical building *(above)* was designed by Sir Frank Baines in 1929–30. In 1994 it became the new home to the British Security Service, MI5.

WESTMINSTER

Lambeth Bridge – Westminster Bridge 920m

After the last Ice Age, the River Tyburn formed a small delta in the marshland before reaching the Thames. The first settlements were founded on a gravel outcrop within the delta, probably for reasons of defence. It became known as Thorney Island and it is here that Westminster Abbey and the Houses of Parliament now stand. This section of the walk goes through the very heart of British Government, Monarchy and Church.

The Houses of Parliament

This building, along with its clock tower 'Big Ben', has come to symbolise London. There has been a royal palace on this site since the reign of Edward the Confessor (1042–66). Following a fire in 1263, Henry III rebuilt the palace and made it the centre of his government, and it became the prime residence for the English monarchy. Access to the river was key for communication and transport. A second fire in 1512 forced the removal of the monarch to the Palace of Whitehall further north on the river. Parliament now met in what remained of the old royal palaces. The Westminster Palace, as it was still known, grew haphazardly, with no real planning. It was not the grandiose structure we see today. A third fire in 1834 destroyed most of the buildings except for Westminster Hall (built by William II in 1099) with its magnificent hammerbeam roof. A debate raged over how the new Parliament should look. Following a competition which saw nearly a hundred entries, the Gothic Revivalists won the day. The new building was created by Sir Charles Barry and Augustus W.N. Pugin. Pugin was just twenty-three when he started work on the interior, designing every detail down to the coat hangers and inkwells. The entire structure is 287m long and was positioned on the banks of the Thames as a defensive measure insisted upon by the Duke of Wellington. Today, the river immediately adjacent to Parliament is off-limits to shipping.

Right: Henry Moore's Knife Edge Two-Piece *1962–65.*
Below right: Auguste Rodin's The Burghers of Calais *(in Victoria Tower Gardens).*

Millbank

Victoria Tower Gardens

Buxton Drinking Fountain

This fountain *(left, no longer working)* was commissioned by Charles Buxton MP, son of Thomas Buxton, who along with William Wilberforce, was largely responsible for the abolition of slavery throughout the British Colonies. It was originally sited in Parliament Square in 1865, and later moved, in 1949 to Victoria Tower Gardens. However, this fabulous Gothic Revival structure really has very little to do with abolitionism.

ON THE OTHER BANK
Lambeth Palace page 78

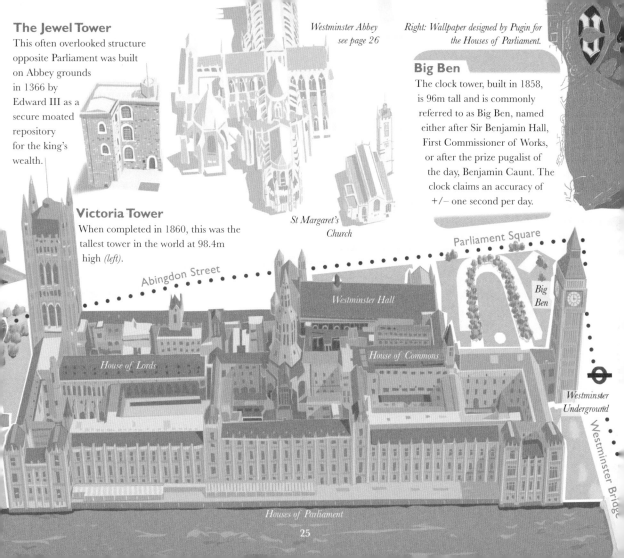

The Jewel Tower

This often overlooked structure opposite Parliament was built on Abbey grounds in 1366 by Edward III as a secure moated repository for the king's wealth.

Westminster Abbey see page 26

Right: Wallpaper designed by Pugin for the Houses of Parliament.

Big Ben

The clock tower, built in 1858, is 96m tall and is commonly referred to as Big Ben, named either after Sir Benjamin Hall, First Commissioner of Works, or after the prize pugalist of the day, Benjamin Caunt. The clock claims an accuracy of +/− one second per day.

Victoria Tower

When completed in 1860, this was the tallest tower in the world at 98.4m high *(left)*.

St Margaret's Church

Parliament Square

Abingdon Street

Westminster Hall

Big Ben

House of Lords

House of Commons

Westminster Underground

Westminster Bridge

Houses of Parliament

Poet's Corner

Poet's Corner, located in the south transept of Westminster Abbey, is so called because of the large number of writers, poets and playwrights that are buried or commemorated there. The first writer interred here was Geoffrey Chaucer in 1400. Nearly seventy notables are buried in Poet's Corner (and around the Abbey), including Robert Browning, Charles Dickens, Thomas Hardy, Ben Jonson, Rudyard Kipling, Alfred Lord Tennyson and the composers George Frideric Handel and Henry Purcell. Those honoured, but not interred here, include the Brontë sisters, William Shakespeare, William Blake, John Betjeman, Samuel Taylor Coleridge, Jane Austen, Ted Hughes, John Keats, Edward Lear, Christopher Marlowe, Walter Scott and Oscar Wilde. Space for more is rapidly diminishing, and even the stained glass windows are being consumed with memorials. Other well known people buried here include Isaac Newton, Charles Darwin, and the slave trade abolitionist William Wilberforce. The Abbey houses one of the most impressive collections of tombs and memorials in the world: a thousand-year 'Who's Who' of notable Britons.

Left: The west façade of Westminster Abbey.
Below: The death mask of Oliver Cromwell.

WILLIAM SHAKESPEAR
BURIED AT STRATFO

The first condition of
GEORGE
ELIOT
Mary An
Evans
1819-1
Buried at
the second

Oliver Cromwell

The funeral of Oliver Cromwell, the puritan and commonwealth leader, took place in the abbey in 1658 and his body was briefly interred here. Following the restoration of the monarchy, what was believed to Cromwell's body was exhumed in 1661 and posthumously hung at Tyburn. His severed head remained on a pole at Westminster Hall for twenty-four years.

Coronations, Marriages and Deaths

With the exception of Edward V and Edward VIII, all English and later British monarchs since 1066 have been crowned at the Abbey. Numerous monarchs are buried here, including Edward the Confessor, Edward II, Edward III, Henry V and Elizabeth I. This trend for royal interment within the Abbey ceased in the eighteenth century. Since the beginning of the twentieth century there have been ten royal weddings here.

Right: The gilt-bronze tomb of Henry III, founder of the current Abbey. Left: George Eliot's memorial stone at Poet's Corner.

Tomb of the Unknown Warrior

The body of an unidentified British soldier of the First World War was exhumed from a French battlefield and reburied by the west door in November 1920 as a tribute to all who were killed in the war *(below)*.

BENEATH THIS STONE RESTS THE BODY
OF A BRITISH WARRIOR
UNKNOWN BY NAME OR RANK
BROUGHT FROM FRANCE TO LIE AMONG
THE MOST ILLUSTRIOUS OF THE LAND

WESTMINSTER ABBEY

There has been a place of worship on this site for over a thousand years. In this glorious piece of medieval architecture nearly every English and British monarch has been crowned. The Abbey has become the epitome of the union between the monarchy and the state.

The Beginning

It is not certain who first established a religious institution on this site. The first Christian King of the East Saxons, Sæbert (604–16) may have founded a Benedictine monastery, St Peter's Abbey, on the site of what is now Westminster Abbey. Sæbert has a tomb within the present Abbey. However, archaeologists have recently found a body in Essex which they believe to be Sæbert. Under the reign of King Edgar (959–75), the Abbey received rights to the land over what is now the West End of London, and founded a monastery with twelve monks. The area was originally named West Mynstre as opposed to East Mynstre, the religious settlement on Ludgate Hill – now the site of St Paul's Cathedral. In the 1040s, Edward the Confessor began the process of building the Abbey, in the Romanesque style. He died in 1066 and was the first monarch to be buried within the newly consecrated Westminster Abbey. In the thirteenth century, much of the Abbey was rebuilt by Henry III (1215–72) in honour of the now canonised St Edward the Confessor. Several new structures were added at this time, including the chapter house. This medieval structure is largely what we view today. As with many large churches of this period, the building took several hundred years to complete, and the style of design varied as the work progressed. During the reign and Reformation of Henry VIII, Westminster Abbey was spared dissolution and destruction as he gave it cathedral status. After Henry's death, Mary I turned it back into a Catholic Benedictine Abbey. The two western towers were finally added in 1745. These were designed by Nicholas Hawksmoor, a student of Christopher Wren.

Westminster Bridge

Prior to 1750 there were only two Thames crossings in central London: the Old London Bridge and the new Putney Bridge. The next was in Kingston-upon-Thames, 22km away. Westminster Bridge, with its fifteen piers, was built over the site of an ancient ford crossing. The Thames at that time was much wider and shallower and at low water the river could be forded. The ferrymen, whose livelihoods depended upon the crossing point, lobbied hard to stop the bridge being built. However, the Parliamentary Act was passed and the ferrymen were compensated for their losses. Within a hundred years the foundations of the first bridge were badly affected by water erosion and tide. A replacement bridge was designed by Thomas Page with the architect of the Houses of Parliament, Sir Charles Barry, as consultant. The bridge had to blend in with its Gothic Revival neighbour. It was opened in 1862 on the forty-third birthday of Queen Victoria. The bridge is painted green to reflect the colour of the benches in the House of Commons.

Portcullis House

The Houses of Parliament have become too small to accommodate the growing army of assistants, secretaries and researchers that MPs and Lords require. In 2001 Portcullis House opened across the road from Parliament. It provides office space for over 200 MPs.

Palace of Whitehall

This large area of land from Westminster to Trafalgar Square has been built on by royalty, government and religious bodies over the past 800 years. It was, and still is, a hotchpotch of palaces, offices and houses that despite several attempts was never architecturally unified. The Banqueting Hall on Whitehall *(right)*, designed by Inigo Jones, has survived. It was through one of these windows that Charles I was taken to be executed in 1649.

The Ministry of Defence

The cellars of Henry VIII are enclosed within the basement of this building. In the garden, there are steps created by Wren, which led from the former palace to the river before the Embankment was built. They are now 70m away from the river.

Left: Portcullis House. Below left: Westminster Bridge. Below: Battle of Britain Monument on the Embankment. Right: The Boudica statue.

Whitehall

Westminster Underground

Bridge St.

Victoria Embankment

Westminster Pier

THE B...

OF BRITAIN

Westminster Bridge

Above: Banqueting Hall.

VICTORIA EMBANKMENT
Westminster Bridge – Hungerford Bridge 655m

The Embankment was built as part of the response to improve drastically the sewage system of the capital and the flow of the Thames. A vast amount of human waste was being discharged into the river via streams and ancient sewers. Cholera epidemics had been rife in the early 1800s. Following the 1862 Parliamentary Act, Sir Joseph Bazalgette *(see page 30)* was commissioned to overhaul London's sewerage system. A huge series of interceptor sewers were created to prevent effluent from reaching the Thames. The Victoria Embankment was part of this scheme. All the riverside buildings were removed, including the Cannon Coal Wharf, to make way for the granite slabs and broad boulevard that would become the Embankment that we now see. Beneath the Embankment lie the Northern Low Level Sewer and the Circle and District lines. As a result of this work the width of the river was dramatically reduced.

Right: Charing Cross station. Below: Hungerford Railway Bridge.

Queen Mary Steps

Horse Guards Avenue

Whitehall Gardens

Northumberland Avenue

Victoria Embankment

ON THE OTHER BANK
The former County
Hall page 82

The Boudica Statue
Located on Westminster Bridge and unveiled in 1902 *(left)*, Boudica was leader of the Iceni tribe and organiser of a revolt against the Roman occupation in AD 60.

SIR JOSEPH BAZALGETTE

Not since the last glacier had the London Thames been so radically resculpted. Although most of his work goes unseen, Sir Joseph Bazalgette was one of the great Victorian civil engineers, contributing greatly to the health of Londoners.

A Stinking Capital

Between 1801 and 1841, London's population had doubled to 2 million. With such rapid growth came a major sewage problem. Most human effluence, factory waste and dead animals were being deposited into streams and sewers that ended up in the Thames. The vast majority of Londoners who couldn't access safe, clean water, still extracted their water from the Thames for drinking and washing in. London also had, at this time, over 200,000 cesspits. The Thames shoreline in central London consisted of mud banks of sewage at low tide, which stank in warm weather.

Clockwise from the left: diseased fish in the Thames. Sir Joseph Bazalgette with sewer pipe cross section. Plan of the 1859 sewerage system. Egyptian bench by the Thames. Abbey Mills Pumping Station.

London saw several cholera epidemics in the earlier part of the nineteenth century. In the 1849 outbreak 14,000 died from the infection. Dr John Snow, following his research, showed that cholera was water-borne and not air-borne as had previously been thought. A water pump in Broad Street (now Broadwick Street), Soho, was shown to have been the source of the local outbreak. The pump was only a metre away from an old cesspit.

Even before the 1850s, many had realised that untreated sewage could not simply be dumped into the Thames. The biblical scene painter John Martin had proposed an interceptor sewer in the earlier part of the nineteenth century. However, there was great resistance from owners of business properties lining the river. In 1855, the Metropolitan Board of Works was formed with the sole aim of overhauling the sewage system. Joseph Bazalgette was its chief engineer. Three years later, following sittings of the Commons being suspended as a result of the vile stench emitting from the river, a greater urgency was placed on cleaning up

the Thames. Paddle boats were unable to navigate the river because of the density of floating sewage. The minds of the MPs became focused on acting to eradicate the problem. Bazalgette proposed a huge network of sewerage interceptor pipes.

The Interceptor Sewer

There were 160km of brick-lined, main interceptor pipes built between 1859 and 1865 in London. These were fed by 725km of mains sewers and many thousands of kilometres of existing small local sewers and streams. The network would clear nearly 2 million litres of sewage daily. Using gravity, the sewage would flow from west to east and feed into the treatment works at Beckton, north of the Thames and Plumstead in the south. Pumping stations were required at certain points along the network, such as at Grosvenor Road *(see page 20)* to lift the sewage to a higher-level interceptor pipe leading to Abbey Mills in Stratford. It was thought that the sewage could be safely disposed of on the ebb tide into the estuary. The work for this massive task was paid for by an increase in tax on coal and wine.

In 1864, work began to create the new Victoria Embankment between Westminster and Blackfriars. The Thames was being narrowed and canalised, to improve the tidal flow and flush the river more efficiently.

Above ground, the Victoria Embankment provided a new low-level carriageway linking Westminster to the City. Below this, an underground railway line was also created alongside the sewer. It forms part of what is the District and Circle line today. Much of the reclaimed land became gardens that line the river. The Victoria Embankment opened in 1870. The vast granite shoreline seemed fitting for what was the heart of the British Empire.

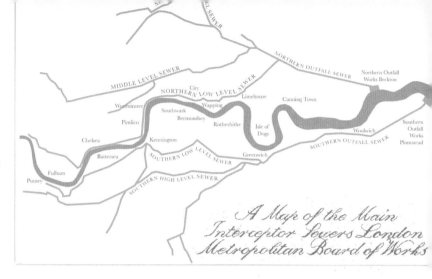

A Map of the Main Interceptor Sewers London Metropolitan Board of Works

The Man who Chained the River

Bazalgette was not only responsible for overhauling the antiquated sewage system; he also created two other embankments and a series of bridges. The Albert Embankment, which opened in 1869, did not carry an interceptor pipe but was built to protect Lambeth from flooding. Chelsea Embankment did include an interceptor sewage pipe. It opened in 1874.

The bridges Bazalgette designed were replacements for existing ones: Battersea Bridge (1887), Putney Bridge (1886) and Hammersmith Bridge (1890). He also proposed plans for Tower Bridge, the Blackwall Tunnel and the Woolwich Free Ferry. Only his plans for the latter were accepted. He also developed plans for Charing Cross Road and Northumberland Avenue. He was knighted in 1874 and died in 1891 in Wimbledon.

His memorial can be found by the riverbank looking sternly up Northumberland Avenue. Inscribed are the words 'Flumini vincula posuit' (He placed chains upon the river). This was a claim of the pharaohs. It is not surprising that the benches along the Embankment feature designs of camels and sphinxes *(right)*.

Charing Cross Station

This railway station stands on the site of the old Hungerford produce market (1682–1862). Once the Old London Bridge was removed in 1831, this used to include a fish market, as fishing boats could travel further upstream to sell their catch. Charles Dickens, as a boy, worked in a boot-blacking factory very close to the market.

The station opened in 1864 and brought rail travel directly into the West End of London. In 1991 the railway shed was completely redesigned and rebuilt by architect Terry Farrell. It now includes office and retail space above the station platforms.

York House Watergate

This portal *(left)*, standing in the Victoria Embankment Gardens, was created in 1626 and once acted as a gate on to the river. Since the Embankment was built, it now stands some 130m away from the Thames.

Victoria Embankment Gardens

Hungerford Bridge

The original crossing here was a suspension footbridge created by Isambard Kingdom Brunel in 1845 to enable access to the Hungerford Market from the south. However, the market struggled to compete with its nearby rival in Covent Garden. When it closed, the London and Brighton Railway acquired the land to build a new station at Charing Cross, and the bridge was removed to make way for a stronger rail crossing. This was designed by the engineer Sir John Hawkshaw and opened in 1864. As a testament to his engineering skills, it is still in use today. The low linear structure has few

adornments and is not the most attractive. The one saving feature of the bridge was the footpaths that were added to each side of the rail bridge. In 1996 plans were created by the architects Lifschutz Davidson to revamp the footbridges and in the process mask the ugly rail crossing. A series of white cantilevered struts hold the cables that carry the footbridges. They opened in 2002, and offer great views of the river and the immediate buildings and monuments lining the Thames. They are also known as the Golden Jubilee bridges.

Hungerford foot and railway bridges, with Charing Cross station behind.

Embankment Underground

Victoria Embankment

Embankment Pier

VICTORIA EMBANKMENT GARDENS

Hungerford Bridge – Waterloo Bridge 460m

Following Bazalgette's embankment of the river, much of the reclaimed land was turned into gardens. The most well known of these is Victoria Embankment Gardens. Previously, many of the palaces and mansions in this area backed directly on to the river. The wealthy owners – archbishops and aristocrats – were situated halfway between the mercantile City of London and the religious and political centre of Westminster, with the river offering the quickest and safest route between the two. In December 1878, Victoria Embankment became the first street in Britain to be permanently lit by electricity.

Right: Shell Mex House was the original London headquarters for Shell Petroleum. The clockface 'Big Benzene' is the largest in London.

Cleopatra's Needle

This 18m pink granite obelisk was a gift from the Viceroy of Egypt to George IV in 1819 as a memorial to Admiral Nelson's Battle of the Nile. It was not brought to London until 1878. On its journey six men died in the Bay of Biscay attempting to recover the 'Needle' after it broke free from the ship towing it. Despite its name, it was built for Pharaoh Tuthmose III (in 1475 BC) and not for Cleopatra.

Savoy Place

Victoria Embankment

The Savoy Hotel

The Count of Savoy was donated land by the Thames by his relative Henry III and in 1263 the Savoy Palace was built. After its demolition during the Peasants Revolt in 1381, it became a hospital for the 'poor and needy' of London. In 1880, Richard D'Oyly Carte constructed the Savoy Theatre to perform Gilbert and Sullivan operas. The profits from these productions enabled him to build the Savoy Hotel *(above)* adjacent to the theatre. It opened in 1889 and was the first hotel in the world to be illuminated by electricity.

ON THE OTHER BANK
The Royal Festival Hall
page 84

ROYAL FESTIVAL HALL

Waterloo Bridge

TEMPLE

Waterloo Bridge –
Blackfriars Bridge 970m

The walk continues along the busy Victoria Embankment and past the very heart of the English legal profession. The curve in the Thames offers some fantastic river views in both directions and of the South Bank on the opposite shore.

Somerset House

Victoria Embankment

Waterloo Bridge

Temple

In the twelfth century this site was the English headquarters of the powerful and influential Knights Templar. The knights were actively involved in the Crusades and protected pilgrims as they journeyed to and from the Holy Land. Following their disbandment in 1312 and later a prohibition against the training of lawyers within the City of London, the Temple became home to the legal profession. The Middle and Inner Temples today form two of the four Inns of Court. The Temple Stairs provided the lawyers and barristers with access to the river and to Westminster Hall and Whitehall. This area has become the centre of English law and a great many barristers' chambers and solicitors offices are located here, with the Royal Courts of Justice to the north. Temple is an anachronism sited within a major world capital. This collection of streets and parks shows very few marks of the twenty-first century. With little traffic, it has a quiet serenity to it.

Middle Temple Hall ▽

🔴 *Temple Underground*

Somerset House

In the sixteenth century, this area was occupied by a Tudor palace, home to Edward Seymour, the Duke of Somerset. After his death in 1658, Oliver Cromwell's body lay in state here. Despite the palace's renovation at the hands of Sir Christopher Wren, by the 1770s the house was neglected and declined and was eventually demolished. The current building, designed by William Chambers, opened in 1801 to house several government departments. The Admiralty offices were located on the riverfront and boats could pass directly into the building *(below left)*. Since the Embankment was created, the river gate is now 40m away from the Thames. The gate can still be seen from the north footpath on Victoria Embankment. The national Register of Births, Marriages and Deaths was established here in 1837, along with what was to become the Inland Revenue. By the late twentieth century, most of the Government's institutes had moved out. Today, Somerset House is home to the Courtauld Institute of Art and the central courtyard is used for concerts and, in winter, ice skating.

ON THE OTHER BANK: OXO Tower page 87

◁ Temple Church

△

Inner Temple Hall

Inner Temple Gardens

Victoria Embankment

Temple Stairs

Blackfriars Pier

River Fleet

The River Fleet is probably London's most famous hidden river. Its source is some 8km to the north-west on Hampstead Heath *(left)*. As the population of London grew from the seventeenth century onwards, the river became increasingly polluted as waste and detritus were discarded into it. Sir Christopher Wren had plans to canalise the lower part of the Fleet but these never materialised. Eventually it was culverted. The Fleet emerges under Blackfriars Bridge and the sluice gate can only be viewed only at low tide.

Unilever House

The building *(right)* stands on what was the old Bridewell Palace. The curvature of Unilever House follows the original mouth of the River Fleet as it enters the Thames.

Blackfriars Bridge

The first bridge, which opened in 1769, was designed by the young and inexperienced architect Robert Mylne. It was an Italianate-style crossing, with ten piers, inspired by Mylne's teacher Piranesi. In 1831, the demolition of the Old London Bridge caused the upstream river speed to increase, which damaged the piers of Blackfriars Bridge. By the mid-1800s the bridge was not wide enough to cope with the growing traffic of central London. Joseph Cubitt, who had designed the adjacent rail bridge, was appointed to create the new Blackfriars Bridge. The ebb and flow of the river dictated the five piers of the replacement bridge had to correspond to those of the rail bridge. The bridge was opened in 1869 by Queen Victoria, on the same day she opened Holborn Viaduct some 350m to the north of the bridge. In 1907 it was widened to carry yet more traffic and is still the widest of all the London bridges. In 1982 the Italian banker Roberto Calvi was found hanging under the bridge (see page 103).

Below: Blackfriars Bridge.
Right: A detail of a pier.

The Black Friar

This narrow wedge of brick and marble *(left)* is a public house that was erected in 1883 and was redesigned by H. Fuller Clark in 1905 in the Arts and Crafts style. More than

fifty types of marble line the interior with carved friezes of monks at work *(above)*. The pub sits on the former site of a Dominican friary. The monks were noted for their black cloaks worn over their habits, hence the name Black Friars. It was possibly here in 1528 that a meeting took place of the Papal delegation and Henry VIII to discuss his divorce from Catherine of Aragon: a process that would ultimately see England breaking away from the Roman Catholic church.

Blackfriars station

St Paul's Cathedral

The current structure *(right)* was designed in the restrained English Baroque style by Sir Christopher Wren and constructed between 1675 and 1711. The Portland stone-clad cathedral and its dome would come to dominate and symbolise the London skyline for centuries. At 111m high, it was the tallest building in London until it was superseded by Millbank Tower *(page 23)* in 1963. The dome and lantern, inspired by St Peter's Basilica in Rome, are open to the public and provide great views over the capital. The cathedral's predecessor had been destroyed by the Great Fire in 1666, and had a spire that was 149m high until it was destroyed by lightning in 1561. St Paul's largely survived the aerial bombardment of the Second World War, though it is possible the German Luftwaffe used the cathedral for navigational purposes. The funerals of Lord Horatio Nelson, The Duke of Wellington, and Sir Winston Churchill all took place here. Fittingly, Wren is buried within his own cathedral, with a tomb inscription in Latin that translates as:

'Reader, if you seek his monument, look around you.'

Right: St Paul's Cathedral.
Near right: The City of London School.
Left: Mermaid Theatre.

White Lion Hill

ON THE OTHER BANK
Tate Modern
page 90

Blackfriars Bridge

Blackfriars station and Railway Bridge

Blackfriars Underpass

ST PAUL'S

Blackfriars Bridge – Southwark Bridge 930m

The Thames Path finally departs the dual carriageway and continues along the bend in the river without the roar of Embankment traffic. Once the steps of the Millennium Bridge are reached, the dome of the great cathedral, St Paul's is finally revealed, between an architectural canyon.

St James Garlickhythe

This is yet another church designed by Wren following the Great Fire of London. It was consecrated in 1682 and became known as 'Wren's Lantern' *(right)*, as the design allowed so much light to enter the church. In the Middle Ages it had been used by pilgrims as a stopping off point *en route* to Santiago da Compostela in Spain. The name Garlickhythe is taken from the once nearby landing stages for garlic and wine from France. The church houses the 300-year-old mummified remains of an unknown person referred to as 'Jimmy Garlick', though he is no longer on public display.

Upper Thames Street

Vintners' Hall

A Vintners' Hall has stood on this site since 1446. The Vintners were a powerful liveried company who controlled the import and export of wine into and out of England. They were one of the twelve great liveried companies of London.

Queenhithe

Queenhithe

This small dock was created sometime prior to AD 890 and was originally the landing place of Aethelred, son-in-law of King Alfred. It was named Queenhithe after Queen Matilda, wife of Henry I, in 1237. (A 'hithe' is a landing place or port.) Although the dock is still preserved, during the 1970s sadly permission was given to demolish the old wharf buildings and a hotel was constructed in its place.

Millennium Bridge

Southwark Bridge

WALBROOK

Southwark Bridge – London Bridge 493m

The walk, well away from motor traffic, passes close to the heart of the City of London and over a small river that contributed to the founding of the capital city. However very little remains of an earlier waterside London along this part of the path.

River Walbrook

All that is visible of the Walbrook, as it enters the Thames, is a metal drain cover and a stone chute: a modest tribute to the stream that is partially responsible for the foundation of London. The Walbrook is the shortest London river and runs between Ludgate Hill, on which St Paul's Cathedral now sits and Cornhill to the east. It is probably one of the major reasons why the Romans chose to build a settlement on this location. The source of the river is about 2km to the north-east in Shoreditch and is now culverted for its entire length.

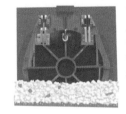

Above: River Walbrook sluice gate.
Below: Walbrook Wharf.

Walbrook Wharf

A working wharf is a rarity in London. This wharf, owned by the Corporation of London, ships over 3 million tonnes of refuse from the City in containers downstream to an energy conversion plant in Bexley. The path is closed when containers are being loaded and unloaded.

Southwark Bridge

By the 1810s the traffic over London and Blackfriars Bridge was so great that a new bridge was needed to alleviate the pressure. John Rennie, who also designed London and Waterloo bridges in the early nineteenth century, was commissioned to create a new bridge across the Thames to connect the City with Southwark. It was a three-span cast-iron construction and was the first London bridge to be illuminated with gas lights. It opened in 1819 and, like many other bridges, a toll was charged. Just over 100 years later in 1921, a wider replacement bridge was created that would allow trams to cross over. It is now the least-used bridge in central London.

Subterranean River Walbrook

Queen Street

Southwark Bridge

Cannon Street Railway Bridge

Fishmongers' Hall

The Worshipful Company of Fishmongers has been in existence for over 700 years and located on this site by London Bridge since 1434. It controlled the number of fishing boats unloading catches in the City and the price of fish. Although today it manages a property portfolio and is an educational charity, it still supports research into matters relating to fish and fishing in the UK. Probably its most famous member was Sir William Walworth, the Mayor of London, who in 1381 killed Wat Tyler and ended the Peasants' Revolt.

Monument Underground

Below: Fishmongers' Hall.

Cannon Street Station

This station, designed by Sir John Hawkshaw and Sir John Wolfe Barry (who also built Hungerford and Blackfriars rail bridges respectively), was opened in 1866 on the site of the Roman Governor's Palace. It brought the railway into the City of London. The twin towers facing the river were 'a tribute' to the church spires created by Wren and they held water tanks to operate the station's hydraulic lifts. The rail bridge was originally named after the Danish Princess Alexandra, who married Edward, Prince of Wales, in 1863. A pedestrian footbridge was originally added, though this was later removed and never restored. Following damage during the Second World War, the station was rebuilt in the 1960s. A decade later the bridge was reduced in width and the original bridge replaced.

King William Street

All that remains of the Old Swan Pier are these wooden stumps, visible only at low water.

London Bridge

ON THE OTHER BANK
Southwark Cathedral
page 93

Christopher Wren was born in Wiltshire in 1632, just ten years before the outbreak of the English Civil War. His father was Dean of Windsor and had clear Royalist connections, which placed the family in some danger. The young Wren was packed off to study at Wadham College, Oxford, as the town had become the royal court and stronghold. By the age of eighteen, Wren had gained his first degree. Six years later he had become Professor of Astronomy at Gresham College, London. Wren, the polymath, was also studying mechanics, philosophy, anatomy and geometry.

In 1660, following the end of the Civil War, and advent of the Restoration, the Royal Society was formed for the advancement of scientific knowledge. Wren was among its founder members, and twenty years later would become it president. It was at this time that Wren began to take an interest in architecture. He received a commission from his uncle for a new chapel at Pembroke College, Cambridge, and from Gilbert Sheldon, the Warden of All Souls, Oxford, to design a structure as a parting gift to the college. In his capacity of Bishop of London, Sheldon also commissioned Wren to produce a plan to restore the crumbling, Gothic St Paul's Cathedral. Influenced by an extended trip to Paris, where Wren saw several new church domes and met numerous influential architects, he submitted his proposals just a week before the Great Fire of London in September 1666 (see page 42).

The Great Fire saw two thirds of the City razed to the ground. Wren was soon appointed as one of three Royal Commissioners to oversee the rebuilding of London. In this role he rapidly drew up Baroque plans for a new City, with streets radiating from piazzas, and even the canalisation of the River Fleet. Too much vested interest, however, saw that these plans never received Royal Assent.

Within the City, eighty-seven churches had been destroyed, of which fifty-two were scheduled to be rebuilt. Ten years after the fire, Wren was overseeing twenty-six church rebuilds, including St Paul's. Much of the rebuilding was paid for by a tax of one shilling (5p) placed on each tonne of coal shipped into the

1   2   3   4   5   6

City. Wren was assisted in this mammoth undertaking by Robert Hooke and Edward Woodroffe. He was very reliant upon their architectural expertise and organisation. In his later working years, he had John Vanbrugh and Nicholas Hawksmoor as assistants. These groups worked closely with the masons, stone cutters and carpenters in the day-to-day running of the projects. Wren had gone from enthusiastic amateur to master architect, with the Great Fire acting as the catalyst.

In 1669, Wren was appointed as Surveyor of the King's Works. This included all the royal palaces, including Hampton Court, Windsor, Chelsea, Kensington, Whitehall, and Greenwich, nearly all of which were connected by the Thames. Wren would go on to oversee

SIR CHRISTOPHER WREN

Wren is one of the most famous British architects. For 300 years, his work dominated the skyline of London, with a sea of church spires, a cathedral and a column.

many developments of these structures *(see pages 18 and 110)*. In 1673 he was knighted for his services.

Even as the foundations were being laid for the new St Paul's Cathedral, the final details including the prospect of a dome, were still being discussed by craftsmen, architects, the church, and the king.

The stone for the cathedral, mainly from the Isle of Portland, was brought up the Thames by ship. The construction of the dome itself was dogged with problems. However, Wren felt it was vital to complete this section early as

an advertisement that would attract interest and funding for the rest of the project. It took thirty-five years to complete the cathedral. Wren is only one of a very few architects to have overseen the entire construction of a cathedral within his own lifetime. The dome of St Paul's would influence the design of many other structures, including the US Capitol, Washington DC.

Wren was married twice, and produced four children. He outlived both his wives and died at the age of ninety-one. He is buried within the crypt of St Paul's Cathedral.

Wren's cathedral, monument and a few churches.
Left to right:
(Sir Christopher Wren)
1   *St Michael Paternoster Royal*
2   *St Martin-within-Ludgate*
3   *St Benet*
4   *St James Garlickhythe*
5   *St Margaret Lothbury*
6   *St Magnus the Martyr*
7   *St Paul's Cathedral*
8   *St Clement Danes*
9   *St Stephen Walbrook*
10 *The Monument*
11 *St Margaret Patten*
12 *St Mary Abchurch*

Detail: St Paul's Cathedral floor.

The Great Fire of London

During the drought of 1666, the very closely packed, tinder-dry wooden buildings with thatched roofs became extremely vulnerable to fire. The Great Fire started in a baker's shop on Pudding Lane on 2 September 1666 and blazed for four days. The Mayor of London, Sir Thomas Bloodworth's indecisiveness in creating fire breaks by demolishing houses resulted in much of the City being destroyed, and at least 70,000 Londoners were left homeless. During the Fire, many City residents were evacuated across the river by boat, as London Bridge too was engulfed in flames. The death toll was reported to be extremely low, though the deaths of working and middle class people were simply not recorded. Despite the ambitious intentions of several city planners of the period, the new street plan of the City mirrored closely that of pre-Fire London.

Fish Lane

London Bridge

Above: Adelaide House, built in 1925.

St Magnus the Martyr

The original church, founded in the eleventh century on reclaimed land, was, like so many in the area, destroyed by the Great Fire of London and later redesigned by Sir Christopher Wren in 1676. The church's tower is considered to be one of his finest. Thomas Farriner, owner of the Pudding Lane bakery, was a church warden of St Magnus and was buried within what was a temporary church in 1670. St Magnus the Martyr sat beside the approach road to the Old London Bridge and was the first church available to travellers and pilgrims to the City from the south. However, in 1831 the bridge was rebuilt 30m upstream. An annual blessing of the Thames takes place each year in January, with the clergy and parishioners of St Magnus and Southwark Cathedral meeting halfway across London Bridge.

Route to St Magnus and The Monument

Left: Steps up to a raised viewing area overlooking the Thames.

ON THE OTHER BANK
St Olaf House
page 96

The Monument

This Doric column, with its 311 steps to the top, is 61m high and 61m away from Pudding Lane *(marked left with an X)*, the starting point of the Great Fire of London. It was designed by Wren and Robert Hook to commemorate the fire and all who died in it. It is the tallest free-standing stone column in the world.

Old Billingsate Fish Market

This former fish market *(below)* was located here in the Pool of London for over 950 years. Fish would be unloaded onto the wharf and processed for despatch. During the nineteenth century the market was rebuilt three times to increase the market's capacity to handle ever-larger quantities of fish to feed the burgeoning metropolis. The final development on this site, in 1877, was designed in an Italianate style by Horace Jones (who would later design Tower Bridge). The author George Orwell worked at the market during the 1930s. The introduction of the railways and refrigeration saw the gradual decline of fish arriving by river. The market moved, in 1982, to a new location in Canary Wharf, East London. The old fish market building is now used as an exhibition and conference centre.

Custom House

There has been a Custom House on this site since Romans times. The creation of London Bridge created a barrier beyond which sea going vessels could not pass. So the location of an import office downstream from the crossing became vital for collecting duty on behalf of the monarch. The Customs and Excise Boards also attempted to thwart smuggling and seize contraband. Such was its value to the Exchequer that the structure was one of the first to be rebuilt following the Great Fire of London. Unsurprisingly, given the amount of combustible materials, such as alcohol and gunpowder, that were seized and stored here, the building was prone to fire. Wren's design burned down in 1715. The 1828 rebuild by Sir Robert Smirke, complete with fireproof rooms, survives to the present day, despite heavy bombing in 1940. The grandest side of the building, of Portland Stone, faces onto the river. The advent of larger ships and containerisation in the 1960s and 1970s, saw the decline of merchant shipping on the Thames and the traditional role of Custom House. However the building *(below)* is still used as offices for HM Revenue & Customs.

Below left: The Old Billingsgate Market hall and detail of the piscine weather vane.

POOL OF LONDON
London Bridge – Water Lane
470m *(excluding the Monument detour)* The walk, still away from traffic, continues through the City and passes the site of the Old London Bridge. A few of the quayside buildings here remain as they would have appeared a hundred years ago. In 1666, all the property north of the river was erased by the Great Fire of London. The Monument, a memorial to the fire and all who died, is worth a detour up its spiral staircase to the viewing platform.

Water Lane

TOWER OF LONDON

Water Lane – Tower Bridge 635m

This is probably the busiest section of the entire London Thames Path. Tourists arriving by coach, Tube and foot swarm to the Tower of London, the oldest complete structure in the capital. It was built nearly one thousand years ago, following the Norman invasion. The path offers both great views of the Tower of London itself and the adjacent Tower Bridge *(overleaf)*.

Tower Subway

This was the world's first train tunnel under a river. Built by James Henry Greathead and opened in 1870, twelve passengers at a time were hauled 410m, in a carriage, beneath the Thames by a steam-powered cable system. Despite its novelty, it rapidly became unpopular and was converted into a walkway after only three months of operation. When Tower Bridge opened in 1894 the tunnel became totally redundant and it was sold to the London Hydraulic Power Company. All that remains above ground is a small circular access point *(right)*, close to the Tower of London ticket office. The tunnel now houses communication cables and water pipes.

ON THE OTHER BANK
HMS *Belfast* &
City Hall
page 96

The Tower of London

Despite the Norman invasion of England in 1066, William the Conqueror and his armies were still operating within enemy territory and needed to secure the capital. The keep (the White Tower) was built upon a former Roman fortification wall and was initially created using stone imported from Caen, northern France. Work started soon after William's arrival in London. The Tower served as both a stronghold and a palace. The complex of outer and inner defensive walls, towers and moats evolved over the next two centuries and became known collectively as the Tower of London. This started a trend over the next few centuries for royal castles (Windsor and Baynard's) and palaces (Hampton, Richmond, Whitehall, Bermondsey and Greenwich) to be built along the edges of the Thames, as travelling by water was much faster and more secure than by land. Major building developments ceased once the royals, Henry VIII onwards, no longer resided within the Tower. Over the centuries the Tower and grounds has been modified, expanded and developed into the collection of structures and architectural styles that are visible today.

Tower Beach

In 1934, regardless of the risk of disease from the river, a small piece of sandy beach was created for local children to play on.

Tower Millennium Pier

44

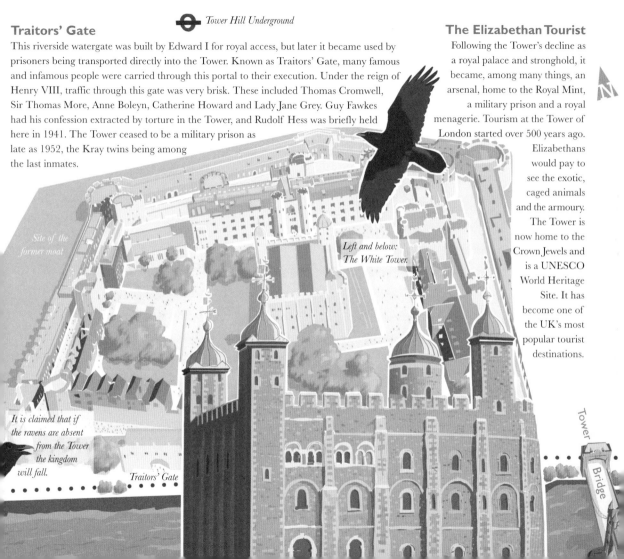

Traitors' Gate

This riverside watergate was built by Edward I for royal access, but later it became used by prisoners being transported directly into the Tower. Known as Traitors' Gate, many famous and infamous people were carried through this portal to their execution. Under the reign of Henry VIII, traffic through this gate was very brisk. These included Thomas Cromwell, Sir Thomas More, Anne Boleyn, Catherine Howard and Lady Jane Grey. Guy Fawkes had his confession extracted by torture in the Tower, and Rudolf Hess was briefly held here in 1941. The Tower ceased to be a military prison as late as 1952, the Kray twins being among the last inmates.

Tower Hill Underground

The Elizabethan Tourist

Following the Tower's decline as a royal palace and stronghold, it became, among many things, an arsenal, home to the Royal Mint, a military prison and a royal menagerie. Tourism at the Tower of London started over 500 years ago. Elizabethans would pay to see the exotic, caged animals and the armoury. The Tower is now home to the Crown Jewels and is a UNESCO World Heritage Site. It has become one of the UK's most popular tourist destinations.

Site of the former moat

Left and below: The White Tower.

It is claimed that if the ravens are absent from the Tower the kingdom will fall.

Traitors' Gate

Tower Bridge

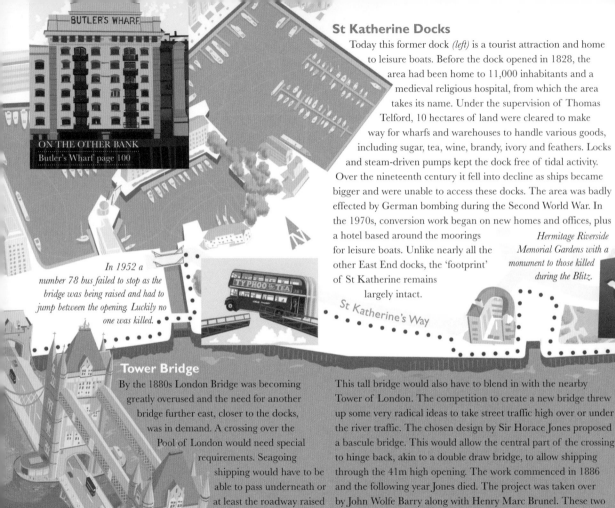

St Katherine Docks

Today this former dock *(left)* is a tourist attraction and home to leisure boats. Before the dock opened in 1828, the area had been home to 11,000 inhabitants and a medieval religious hospital, from which the area takes its name. Under the supervision of Thomas Telford, 10 hectares of land were cleared to make way for wharfs and warehouses to handle various goods, including sugar, tea, wine, brandy, ivory and feathers. Locks and steam-driven pumps kept the dock free of tidal activity. Over the nineteenth century it fell into decline as ships became bigger and were unable to access these docks. The area was badly effected by German bombing during the Second World War. In the 1970s, conversion work began on new homes and offices, plus a hotel based around the moorings for leisure boats. Unlike nearly all the other East End docks, the 'footprint' of St Katherine remains largely intact.

Hermitage Riverside Memorial Gardens with a monument to those killed during the Blitz.

ON THE OTHER BANK
Butler's Wharf page 100

In 1952 a number 78 bus failed to stop as the bridge was being raised and had to jump between the opening. Luckily no one was killed.

St Katherine's Way

Tower Bridge

By the 1880s London Bridge was becoming greatly overused and the need for another bridge further east, closer to the docks, was in demand. A crossing over the Pool of London would need special requirements. Seagoing shipping would have to be able to pass underneath or at least the roadway raised to allow tall ships through.

This tall bridge would also have to blend in with the nearby Tower of London. The competition to create a new bridge threw up some very radical ideas to take street traffic high over or under the river traffic. The chosen design by Sir Horace Jones proposed a bascule bridge. This would allow the central part of the crossing to hinge back, akin to a double draw bridge, to allow shipping through the 41m high opening. The work commenced in 1886 and the following year Jones died. The project was taken over by John Wolfe Barry along with Henry Marc Brunel. These two had previously worked together on Blackfriars Railway Bridge.

London Docks

When the Western Dock, the first part of the London Docks, opened in 1805, it was the closest inland quay to the City of London until St Katherine Docks opened twenty-three years later. Over a period of twenty years, the London Dock expanded several times by adding Tobacco Dock (1813), Hermitage Basin (1821), Eastern Dock (1828) and finally Shadwell Basin (1832). With these new facilities, ships could unload and load in four or five days, whereas previously, shipping stuck in the Thames could wait for a month to discharge its cargo. The London Docks was a very secure, high-walled area, with bonded warehouses for high-value goods such as tobacco, wine, brandy and ivory. The railways never reached London Docks and, as with St Katherine Docks, ever-larger ships were unable to navigate so far up the Thames. Newer, deeper quays were created on the Isle of Dogs further to the east. The Docks finally closed in 1969 and the Western Dock was filled in. In the 1980s a large printworks was built on the site for Rupert Murdoch's News International company. During an industrial dispute between the workers and owners the print works were dubbed 'Fortress Wapping'.

Western Dock

Tobacco Dock

Eastern Dock

Shadwell Basin

Hermitage Basin

LONDON DOCKS
c.1900

Wapping Basin

This page

Page overleaf

Wapping High St

Wapping Old Stairs and The Town of Ramsgate pub

River Police Boatyard

Hermitage Moorings

The steel-framed towers were clad with stone to give it a Gothic Revival appearance and hopefully to blend in with its ancient neighbour. They must have been misguided. Critics of the time hailed it as a sham, saying that it would look better placed next to St Pancras station. The bridge (the eighteenth road crossing over the Thames in London) opened in 1894 and in the first year of operation the bascules were raised 6,000 times. It now opens around 900 times a year. The original hydraulic-powered bascules were converted in 1976 to electric. The upper walkway is now a museum of the bridge.

ST KATHERINE DOCKS

Tower Bridge – Police Boatyard 1,525m

In the sixteenth century this area of marshland east of the Tower of London was drained and protected by a sea wall. Its proximity to the City was invaluable as a connection to the river and the sea beyond. The walk goes through area that has seen nearly two thousand years of merchant trade. Today virtually the entire area has been redeveloped into expensive living quarters and office space.

St John's Old School

The former school on Scandrett Street, founded in 1695, has two Coade stone figures *(left)* above the doors.

The Turks Head

The current building *(left)*, located on the corner of Green Bank and Scandrett Street, was reconstructed in 1927 as a pub with ox-blood exterior tiles and glazed signage. It managed to survive the Blitz. Now no longer a pub, it has been converted into a fine community based café, in contrast to many of the City eateries in the neighbourhood.

Execution Dock

Those found guilty of serious crimes at sea, such as piracy or mutiny, were sentenced by the British Admiralty to death by hanging. The condemned were transported to Execution Dock, on the Thames shore close to what is now Wapping Overground station *(below)*. The condemned prisoners had their last quart of ale at a hostelry, also named The Turks Head, located adjacent to the Thames. They were hung by a short rope that slowly asphyxiated them, rather than breaking their necks. Crowds often gathered in boats to watch the execution. Only after three tides had washed over the dead body could it be cut down. Captain Kidd was hung here in 1701. The pub was destroyed during the Blitz.

Scandrett Street

Green Bank

Marine Police Force

Established in 1798 to reduce the amount of piracy from shipping anchored in the Thames Pool, the Marine Police Force was initially funded by several trading companies, whose cargoes were being pilfered. Headed by Patrick Colquhoun, the Force patrolled the river in rowing boats, boarding ships to check inventories against actual cargoes being loaded and unloaded. For the owners it was an immediate success, and by 1800 the Force was granted Government approval and became a public organisation. It was not popular with a large percentage of the 33,000 men who were working the river and who would lose income if they could no longer steal from the holds. Although the amount of shipping using the Thames has dramatically reduced in the past hundred years, the Marine Police Unit still has a role in patrolling the river and the marine environments within London. It is based on Wapping High Street in the same spot *(below with pier)* where it was founded.

The River Police Boatyard

Built in 1973 *(above left)*, this is a large and unsightly blue-and-white fibreglass structure.

ON THE OTHER BANK
The Leaning Tower of Rotherhithe
page 104

Wapping Street

Top: The sign above the London Overground station. Right: The Execution Dock gibbet. Below: The Overground station with the Thames Tunnel. Below right: New Crane Stairs, with access to the river shoreline.

Wapping High Stre

WAPPING

Police Boatyard – Shadwell Basin 1,252m

A large part of the walk on this section is not within sight of the river, but through the redeveloped Wapping High Street of converted wharves and warehouses. However, there are several stairs down to the river where, at low tide, the shoreline is accessible.

Wapping Hydraulic Power Station

This former hydraulic pumping station, opposite The Prospect of Whitby, was built in 1890 to supply hydraulic power to many of London's theatres, shops, docks and hotels, via 290km of subterranean pipes. The compressed energy, generated by coal and later electricity, was used to power lifts, stage curtains, cranes and the bascules of Tower Bridge *(see page 46)*. Electrical power eventually superseded hydraulic power. The station closed in 1977, leaving some of the power generating equipment in place. It then became home to the Wapping Project, an arts space and restaurant. The future use of the building is under review.

The Prospect of Whitby

There has been a pub on this site for nearly 500 years and it claims to be the oldest riverside pub in London. It was formerly known as *The Pelican* then *The Devil's Tavern*. The current structure *(below right, viewed from Wapping Wall)* was built in the nineteenth century. Samuel Pepys, J.M.W. Turner, 'Hanging' Judge Jeffreys and Charles Dickens have all imbibed at this pub. Turner may have painted *The Fighting Temeraire* (1839) from the rear of this hostelry. The views of the Thames from this spot are spectacular. The current name, adopted in 1777, is taken from a Whitby-registered ship, the *Whitby*, that used to moor close by.

London Hydraulic Power Company 1890

Above: The bascule bridge over the Shadwell Basin entrance. Right: St Paul's church. Below left: Wapping Hydraulic Station.

Shadwell Basin

The basin was a part of the London Dock Company expansion eastwards in the 1830s. In 1854–8 it was extended, with a 13.5m entrance to cope with the new, wider ships. The entrance is marked by a bascule lifting bridge, identical to the one on the south shore at the entrance to Surrey Commercial Docks *(see page 106)*. This basin is the only one of the London Docks developments not to have been filled in. Today it is used mainly for water-based recreation.

Wapping Wall

Wapping Wall

A WORD ON THE WATER

The London Thames has always held a special fascination for authors, especially those who lived and worked by the waterside. The river was often the life-blood that pumped through many works of fiction, poems and diaries.

These were not always writings about an idyllic Thames, but often described the working river of the capital: an industrial and foul tidal stream that characters earned an income from, dredged the dead for money or used its decay as metaphor of civilisation.

The sailor, explorer, courtier and spy, Sir Walter Raleigh, (1552–1618) wrote longingly of his adopted home river: 'There are two things scarce matched in the universe: the sun in heaven and the Thames on earth.' The quote can be found incised into the wall by at Montaque Close, north of Southwark Cathedral by the river *(page 93)*.

William Shakespeare (1564–1616) will have crossed the Thames by ferry innumerable times from his home in Blackfriars to the Globe theatre in Southwark. London had only one narrow bridge at this time, London Bridge. He referred to a river's movements in *The Two Gentlemen of Verona*: 'Tut, man, I mean thou'lt lose the flood, and, in losing the flood, lose thy voyage.'

In 1750, the second bridge across the Thames in London was constructed at Westminster. Some fifty years later William Wordsworth, on passing over the bridge early one morning, was moved to write an exhortation: 'Composed upon Westminster Bridge, September 3, 1802'. The sonnet commences with the line 'Earth hath not anything to show more fair' and is a celebration of the huge slumbering giant of the city, about to awake. London was becoming the largest city on earth. However, it was not the London that

William Blake viewed some eight years earlier. In his poem *London* (1794), he wrote:

I wander thro' each charter'd street,
Near where the charter'd Thames does flow.
And mark in every face I meet
Marks of weakness, marks of woe.

He would later write of 'these dark Satanic Mills', a metaphorical reference to the industrial landscape of Lambeth *(see page 79)*. Wordsworth was a tourist, and Blake was a riverside inhabitant of the metropolis.

Charles Dickens (1812–70) returns, in so many of his novels, to the dark, brooding Thames. At a young age, he had worked in a blacking factory by the river at Hungerford Stairs *(see page 32)*. In *David Copperfield* (1850), Dickens describes the river in the following terms: 'Slimy gaps and causeways, winding among old wooden piles, with a sickly substance clinging to the latter, like green hair, and the rags of last year's handbills offering rewards for drowned men fluttering above high-water mark, led down through the ooze and slush to the ebb-tide.' And in *Our Mutual Friend* (1865) Lizzie Hexam enters into this decay, sculling 'a boat of dirty and disreputable appearance', while her father, Gaffer Hexam, keeps a careful eye out for the corpses of the drowned, at night, on the river between Southwark Bridge and London Bridge. The pair made their living by emptying the pockets of the dead.

Arthur Conan Doyle, in *The Sign of Four* (1890), has Sherlock Holmes and Dr Watson pursuing a murderer along the Thames. 'At Blackwall we could not have been more than two hundred and fifty [yards] . . . never did sport give me such a wild thrill as this mad, flying manhunt down the Thames. Steadily we drew in upon them, yard by yard.'

In one of H.G. Wells' (1866–1946) lesser-known novels, *Tono-Bungay* (1909), the character George Ponderevo also charges along the river in his new motorised boat, a destroyer: '[the] X2 went ripping through the dirty oily water . . . past the long stretches of muddy meadow and muddy suburb to Battersea and Chelsea'. Ponderevo is racing along the Thames past to towards a new technological future. 'I remember how I laughed aloud at the glimpse of the name of a London County Council steamboat that ran across me. *Caxton* it was called, and another was *Pepys*, and another was *Shakespeare*.' In his wake, 'The river passes – London passes, England passes.' Was Wells launching his own Futurist agenda for England? The Italian Futurism movement had also been founded in the same year.

No such speed for Jerome K. Jerome (1859–1927). The Thames will have seeped into his consciousness at an early age, as his father ran a business on Narrow Street adjacent to the river at Limehouse Reach. Jerome's best known novel, *Three Men in a Boat* (1889) was set upstream, in the leafy idyll of the Thames between Kingston and Oxford. He was escaping the stink and pollution of the urban river.

The working title of the poem *The Waste Land* (1922) by T.S. Eliot (1888–1965) was *He do the Police in Different Voices*, a line taken from Dickens' *Our Mutual Friend*. This complex and dark Modernist poem, written in numerous voices, is about the decay of culture, and borrows heavily from literature both ancient and modern. The state of the Thames in the early twentieth century acted as an allegory for Eliot's theme.

Under the brown fog of a winter dawn,
A crowd flowed over London Bridge, so many,
I had not thought death had undone so many.

Is this Eliot's vision of Dante's *Inferno* visited upon London Bridge in the 'Unreal City'? Later in the poem, Eliot borrows from Edmund Spenser's nuptial song *Prothalamion* (1596), 'Sweet Thames run softly, till I end my song'. Eliot then reminds us that his river is now polluted

and of how Spenser's unpolluted river appeared in happier times:

The river bears no empty bottles, sandwich papers,
Silk handkerchiefs, cardboard boxes cigarette ends
Or other testimony of summer nights.

John Masefield (1878–1967), the writer, Poet Laureate and sailor, had no such dark visions, after viewing the vast warehouses of the East India Dock Company in 1914. He neatly captured the mercantile nature of the London and the Thames in this poetic celebration of the docks.

You showed me nutmegs and nutmeg husks,
Ostrich feathers and elephant tusks
Hundreds of tons of costly tea
Packed in wood by the Cingalee
And a myriad drugs which disagree
Cinnamon, myrrh and mace you showed
Golden paradise birds that glowed
And a billion cloves in an odorous mount
And choice port wine from a bright glass fount
You showed, for a most delightful hour
The wealth of the world, and London's power.

LIMEHOUSE

Shadwell Basin – Limekiln Dock 1,600m

Until seventy years ago, Limehouse was a district of slums and crime, ship-building and wharves. Since the Second World War, just about everything has changed beyond recognition. Government investment and private development have transformed the district, like many stretches of the Thames, into expensive homes and industries that have precious little to do with the river.

King Edward VII Memorial Park

In 1922 this 3.2 hectare park was opened by George V as an open space for the local population. During the nineteenth century this area had been the location for Shadwell Fish Market. There is a plaque in the park that commemorates Sir Hugh Willoughby's ill-fated expedition, that started from this point in 1553, to find the north-east passage through the Arctic.

Limehouse DLR

A Source of Riches

The name of this area comes from the lime oasts (or kilns) that manufactured quicklime for use in house building. The activity began in the fourteenth century, when chalk, the raw material, was shipped over from Kent. The area was also renowned for ship-building and rope-making. Limehouse became home to many foreign sailors who, once paid off, settled in the area. London's first China Town was established here. As a district of poverty, opium dens and ill-repute, many authors located their fictional characters here: Wilde's Dorian Grey, Conan Doyle's Sherlock Holmes,

Left: The Free Trade Wharf, built in the 1790s for the East India Company to store imported saltpetre.

The Highway

North ventilation shaft for the Rotherhithe Tunnel

Tunnel

Rotherhithe

Rotherhithe Tunnel

By the late nineteenth century there was an urgent need to connect the two large dock facilities north and south of the river. Traffic had been using the overstretched London and Tower Bridges. A bridge with sufficient clearance for shipping and approach ramps was deemed almost impossible, given the amount of residential and warehousing property on either shore, so a single-bore tunnel, 1,480m long, was created and opened in 1908. It was designed for horse-drawn traffic. Such tunnels were never built straight: the bends at either end prevented the horses from seeing the oncoming light, which could cause them to bolt. Ventilation shafts are still visible on each shore *(left)*. The tunnel can still be walked through, but given the volume of motor traffic this is not advisable.

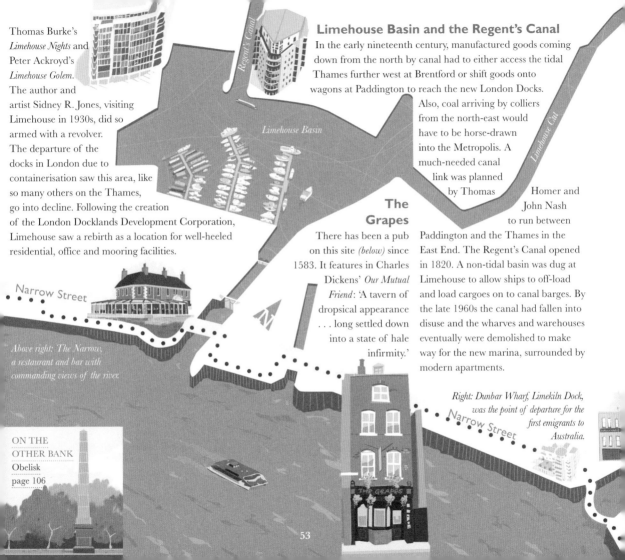

Thomas Burke's *Limehouse Nights* and Peter Ackroyd's *Limehouse Golem*. The author and artist Sidney R. Jones, visiting Limehouse in 1930s, did so armed with a revolver. The departure of the docks in London due to containerisation saw this area, like so many others on the Thames, go into decline. Following the creation of the London Docklands Development Corporation, Limehouse saw a rebirth as a location for well-heeled residential, office and mooring facilities.

Above right: The Narrow, a restaurant and bar with commanding views of the river.

ON THE OTHER BANK
Obelisk
page 106

Limehouse Basin and the Regent's Canal

In the early nineteenth century, manufactured goods coming down from the north by canal had to either access the tidal Thames further west at Brentford or shift goods onto wagons at Paddington to reach the new London Docks. Also, coal arriving by colliers from the north-east would have to be horse-drawn into the Metropolis. A much-needed canal link was planned by Thomas Homer and John Nash to run between Paddington and the Thames in the East End. The Regent's Canal opened in 1820. A non-tidal basin was dug at Limehouse to allow ships to off-load and load cargoes on to canal barges. By the late 1960s the canal had fallen into disuse and the wharves and warehouses eventually were demolished to make way for the new marina, surrounded by modern apartments.

The Grapes

There has been a pub on this site *(below)* since 1583. It features in Charles Dickens' *Our Mutual Friend*: 'A tavern of dropsical appearance . . . long settled down into a state of hale infirmity.'

Right: Dunbar Wharf, Limekiln Dock, was the point of departure for the first emigrants to Australia.

53

Canary Wharf

The rise of containerisation in the 1960s and an increase in ship sizes saw docks in East London fall into decline. To the east, deepwater ports such as Tilbury were able to accommodate the new fleets of merchant vessels. In 1981 the London Docklands Development Corporation was created to renovate the old dock areas. Armed with new planning legislation and tax breaks, they were able to encourage the development of new houses, offices and businesses on a massive scale. A new infrastructure of roads and the Dockland Light Railway were installed. The culmination of this growth was One Canada Square (or Canary Wharf as it is commonly known), at 235m the tallest building in Europe when it opened in 1991. It became the iconic representation of the East London development. Designed by César Pelli & Associates, this stone-clad tower and its high-rise neighbours began to resemble something akin to a small American city. Many international finance companies located here, employing about 90,000 people.

Canary Wharf DLR

Left: The Museuem of London Docklands

Canary Wharf Pier

West India Docks

These docks were developed and opened in 1802, by a wealthy West India merchant and shipowner, Robert Milligan. He and fellow traders were suffering financially as a result of delays and theft from riverside warehouses. Collectively they lobbied Parliament and created a secure, 6m high, walled, non-tidal dock on the Isle of Dogs. With 11km of dockside, it was the largest of its type in the world and could hold up to 600 vessels. A monopoly was initially created, as all trade from the West Indies had to pass through these docks. The docks were built with profits earned through slavery, and even after the Slave Trade Act was passed in 1807, at least twenty-two ships continued to ply the triangular trade: from West India Dock to West Africa to transport slaves to the West Indies and back home again with rum, coffee and sugar.

Museum of London Docklands

Located within the original Georgian West India Quay Warehouses (a Grade I listed building) is a museum devoted to telling the maritime story of London from the Roman settlements to the present day.

ON THE OTHER BANK
Greenland Dock
page 107

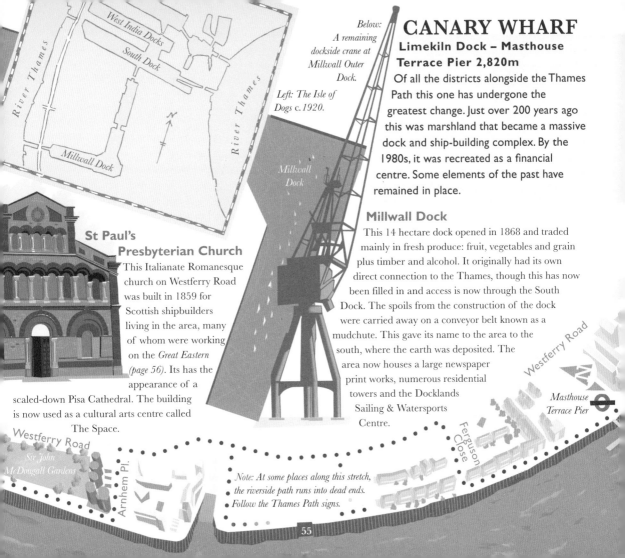

CANARY WHARF

Limekiln Dock – Masthouse Terrace Pier 2,820m

Of all the districts alongside the Thames Path this one has undergone the greatest change. Just over 200 years ago this was marshland that became a massive dock and ship-building complex. By the 1980s, it was recreated as a financial centre. Some elements of the past have remained in place.

Millwall Dock

This 14 hectare dock opened in 1868 and traded mainly in fresh produce: fruit, vegetables and grain plus timber and alcohol. It originally had its own direct connection to the Thames, though this has now been filled in and access is now through the South Dock. The spoils from the construction of the dock were carried away on a conveyor belt known as a mudchute. This gave its name to the area to the south, where the earth was deposited. The area now houses a large newspaper print works, numerous residential towers and the Docklands Sailing & Watersports Centre.

West India Docks

South Dock

River Thames

River Thames

Millwall Dock

Millwall Dock

Below: A remaining dockside crane at Millwall Outer Dock.

Left: The Isle of Dogs c.1920.

St Paul's Presbyterian Church

This Italianate Romanesque church on Westferry Road was built in 1859 for Scottish shipbuilders living in the area, many of whom were working on the *Great Eastern* (page 56). Its has the appearance of a scaled-down Pisa Cathedral. The building is now used as a cultural arts centre called The Space.

Westferry Road

Westferry Road

Sir John McDougall Gardens

Arnhem Pl.

Ferguson Close

Masthouse Terrace Pier

Note: At some places along this stretch, the riverside path runs into dead ends. Follow the Thames Path signs.

ISLAND GARDENS

Masthouse Terrace Pier – Cubitt Wharf 1,840m

The walk continues along the southern tip of the Isle of Dogs. As the river bends, the impressive vista of Greenwich unfolds on the south shore. Like Canary Wharf, the whole area here has transformed from warehouses and manufacturing into expensive residential abodes lining the Thames, plus London's largest urban farm.

Far left: The remains of the Great Eastern *slipway. Left: The former Burrell colour factory. Below: The* Great Eastern. *Right: Isambard Kingdom Brunel.*

Masthouse Terrace Pier

Burrells Wharf

Originally, this was the location of the Russell's shipyard *(see right)*. In 1888, Burrells built a colour factory, which lasted nearly a hundred years. Raw materials were converted into dyes for colouring for the print, paint and plastic industries.

The *Great Eastern*

In 1854, work began on the world's largest ship. It was designed by Isambard Kingdom Brunel at the John Scott Russell shipyard on the Isle of Dogs, and followed the success Brunel had had with other steamships: the *Great Western* and the *Great Britain*. The proposed ship was to be 211m long and had to be built and launched sideways into the Thames. The revolutionary double-skinned hull was propelled by paddles and a single screw propeller, plus sail power. It was planned that the *Great Eastern* would carry 4,000 passengers non-stop to Australia. The ill-fated ship began life with financial problems, which blighted the build, and bankruptcy nearly terminated the project. At the first launch in 1857, the ship, then named *Leviathan*, could not be moved off the slipway and one worker was killed in the process. It took several further attempts to get the ship into the water. In 1859, two days before the maiden voyage, Brunel had a stroke and died ten days later at the age of fifty-three. An explosion on the first voyage killed five of the crew. Despite the original plans, the *Great Eastern* never plied the seas to the Far East; instead, she traversed across the Atlantic. Only thirty-five paying passengers made the initial trip to North America, along with 420 crew. The remainder of the ship's life was riddled with misfortune. On its third voyage the ship hit a storm and lost both paddle wheels and the use of the rudder. The *Great Eastern*, having never made a profit, was sold and became a cable-laying ship before being broken up in 1890. Part of the slipway on the Isle of Dogs still remains.

Westferry Road

Ferry Street

Mudchute Park and Farm

At 13 hectares in size, this is London's largest urban farm, built on reclaimed land with earth dug from the Millwall Dock. The farm has a quiet, remote and rural feel . . . that is, until Canary Wharf looms into view.

Cubitt Wharf

Mudchute Park and Farm

Rope Walk. The site of a former ropemakers' spinning yard.

Millwall Park

Millwall FC

The name Millwall is probably best associated with its football club. However, Millwall FC's ground is some 3km to the south-west, in Bermondsey on the other side of the river. It was founded in 1885 in Millwall, Isle of Dogs, by workers of C&E Morton's canning factory. They had two grounds on Millwall Park. In 1910 they moved across the Thames to a larger ground but retained their name.

Greenwich Foot Tunnel

This 370m foot tunnel under the Thames links Island Gardens with Cutty Sark Gardens to the south. It was designed by Sir Alexander Binnie and opened in 1902 to reduce the pressure on the ferry carrying workers to and from the docks in the Isle of Dogs. Binnie also designed Vauxhall Bridge and the Blackwall Tunnel. It is claimed that in the tunnel at low water you can hear shipping passing overhead. This marks the end of the official Thames Path (north).

Island Gardens DLR

Manchester Road

Left: Entrance to the Greenwich Foot Tunnel.

Island Gardens

ON THE OTHER BANK

Old Royal Naval Hospital page 111

CUBITT TOWN

Cubitt Wharf – Blackwall Basin Entrance 1,900m

The districts of Blackwall and Millwall are listed as some of the most deprived areas in the UK, yet they rub shoulders with Canary Wharf and some of the highest earners in the country. The official Thames Path ends at the Greenwich Foot Tunnel but this book continues on along a river path heading ultimately towards the Thames Barrier Park.

Cubitt Town

Starting in 1842, William Cubitt MP, brother of Thomas Cubitt *(see page 21)* created a small new town complex on this then empty corner of the Isle of Dogs. He laid out an industrial infrastructure that included cement factories, brickyards, asphalt and timber wharves, plus housing, pubs and churches for the workers. He modestly named the district after himself. During the bombing raids of the Second World War, nearly all the houses and factories were destroyed. The wrecked dwellings were replaced by council houses and later with private residences overlooking the Thames. William Cubitt was also responsible for the construction of the first Euston railway station in 1837.

Left: At the riverside memorial to firefighters who died in an explosion in 1969 is Sextant Avenue, a neo-Nash terrace of houses with a crescent at the far end.

Cubitt Wharf

London Dock Strike

Prior to 1889, dockers were recruited on a daily 'call-on' basis. Workers often fought among themselves to be at the head of the throng to acquire employment. Many were seriously injured in the battle for temporary jobs, as men and their families went without food if they didn't work.

Ben Tillett, a trade union organiser, formed the Dock, Wharf, Riverside and General Labourers' Union as a response to the unrest caused by the 'call-on' method of employment. A minor dispute over bonus payments in August 1889 grew into the Dock Strike. 100,000 dockers came out on strike demanding an increase to 6d (2½p) per hour and greater security of employment. With the docks of London closed, and unloaded shipping clogging up the Thames, the owners quickly capitulated and new terms were agreed. It became a milestone in the growth of British labour history. Tillett went on to become Labour MP for Salford North in 1917.

DOCK LABOURERS' STRIKE RELIEF FUND

ON THE OTHER BANK
The O₂ Arena page 114

Isle of Dogs

This peninsula (the subject of this and the previous four pages) was formerly marshland surrounded by the River Thames on three sides. Technically it became an island following the construction of the Limehouse Cut in 1770. Its name is possibly derived from the royal hunting dogs that were kennelled here by Edward III and Henry VIII, or from its drainage dykes ('dogs' being a corruption of 'dykes').

In 1800 it had a population of a dozen. Within a hundred years and the construction of the docks, this had grown to over 21,000, mainly dockers and ship workers. The decline of the docks in the late twentieth century has resulted in an impoverishment of the area, in parts, with abandoned warehouses, factories and houses.

South Dock

Former City Canal

The Blitz

The Docks were a huge economic target for Hitler's Luftwaffe in 1940. At the peak of attacks a 32km column of 1,000 bombers and fighter aircraft rained bombs and incendiaries down upon the East End. These raids lasted for fifty-seven days. The scars of war took many decades to repair.

Blackwall Basin

Pumping station

Preston's Road

The Gun

Isle of Dogs Pumping Station

This unmanned, Egyptian-styled stormwater pumping station was designed by the architect John Outram and came into service in 1988. It was created to prevent the eastern section of Isle of Dogs from flooding in the event of heavy storms. A fusion of bright primary-coloured capitals sit above the short brick-built columns. The Egyptian allusions had been used by Bazalgette, in connection with the river, some 120 years earlier *(see page 31)*.

City Canal

This short cut was built to allow shipping on the Thames to avoid the Isle of Dogs loop, especially if the wind and tide were against them. It opened in 1805 but was a financial failure and was sold to the West India Dock Company to form the South Dock.

The Gun

There has been public house on this site for over 250 years. It is claimed that Lord Nelson would arrange his assignations with Lady Emma Hamilton here. The pub is so named after the cannon that was fired to mark the opening of the West India Docks in 1802. This gastropub has a riverside terrace, with great views along the curving Thames and the O_2 Arena.

The GUN

BLACKWALL

Blackwall Basin Entrance – Lower Lee Crossing Roundabout 3,730m

By East India Dock nature reserve, the redevelopment stops and suddenly you are in a much grittier, industrial part of the river walk. Gone are the glossy high rises of investment banks and their dormitory towers and in come the broken industrial estates and flyovers. However, embedded within this urban detritus are some real surprises.

Docklands Light Railway

The network opened in 1987 as an automatic light rail network to serve the newly formed Docklands area. Since its creation the number of passengers has grown every year and the system has been expanded with more stations and longer platforms to accommodate more cars.

Blackwall DLR

Above: a DLR train.

East India Docks

The East India Company was formed by Royal Charter in 1600 to trade with India and the Far East, specialising in the import of silks, carpets, opium and tea. Following the creation of the West India Dock, the company was eager to establish its own secure, permanent basin. The docks were built and opened in 1806. As with other London docks they suffered at the hands of German bombers in the Second World War and later from containerisation. The dock closed in 1967 and only the entrance now survives *(below right)*, which along with a small wooded area, is now a nature reserve. It forms the southernmost section of the Lee Valley Park.

East India DLR

Blackwall Way

Newport Avenue

The Prime Meridian Walk, marking the 0° longitude line

Biscayne Ave

Providence Wharf

Blackwall Tunnel

East India Dock Basin

Virginia Quay

From this location in December 1606 three ships sailed to North America and would establish the first English settlement at Jamestown, Virginia. A rather brutal memorial with an astrolabe marks the site of their departure.

Preston's Rd

Yabsley St

Blackwall Tunnel

Trinity Buoy Wharf

The peninsula *(right)* formed between the Thames and Bow Creek is somewhat isolated and free of late twentieth century intervention. Until 1988, the wharf was home to the Trinity House workshop. Since the sixteenth century, buoys and lighthouse mechanisms have been built here to assist shipping navigate the British Isles. Michael Faraday had an experimental laboratory here and created the first electrically powered lighthouse. The octagonal lighthouse on the wharf was used to train lighthouse keepers. The lantern has been removed and it is now home to the Longplayer project *(see right)*. The wharf is also now home to a collection of studios, galleries, offices and the Thames Clippers. Bizarrely, a genuine chrome American eatery, Fatboy's Diner is located by the Creek.

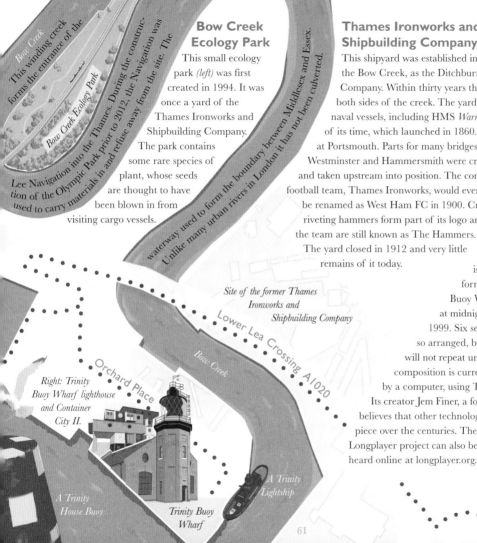

Bow Creek Ecology Park

This small ecology park *(left)* was first created in 1994. It was once a yard of the Thames Ironworks and Shipbuilding Company. The park contains some rare species of plant, whose seeds are thought to have been blown in from visiting cargo vessels.

Bow Creek This winding creek forms the entrance of the Lee Navigation into the Thames. During the construction of the Olympic Park prior to 2012, the Navigation was used to carry materials in and refuse away from the site. The

Bow Creek Ecology Park

waterway used to form the boundary between Middlesex and Essex. Unlike many urban rivers in London it has not been culverted.

Thames Ironworks and Shipbuilding Company

This shipyard was established in 1838 on the banks of the Bow Creek, as the Ditchburn and Mare Shipbuilding Company. Within thirty years the yard expanded to cover both sides of the creek. The yard would produce over 140 naval vessels, including HMS *Warrior*, the largest warship of its time, which launched in 1860. It is now preserved at Portsmouth. Parts for many bridges including Westminster and Hammersmith were created here and taken upstream into position. The company's football team, Thames Ironworks, would eventually be renamed as West Ham FC in 1900. Crossed riveting hammers form part of its logo and the team are still known as The Hammers. The yard closed in 1912 and very little remains of it today.

Site of the former Thames Ironworks and Shipbuilding Company

Lower Lea Crossing A1020

Orchard Place

Bow Creek

Right: Trinity Buoy Wharf lighthouse and Container City II.

A Trinity House Buoy

Trinity Buoy Wharf

A Trinity Lightship

Longplayer

This 1,000-year-long musical composition is running within the former Lighthouse at Trinity Buoy Wharf. The piece began at midnight on 31 December 1999. Six sections of music are so arranged, by algorithm, that they will not repeat until the year 2999. The composition is currently being generated by a computer, using Tibetan singing bowls. Its creator Jem Finer, a founder of The Pogues, believes that other technologies will carry the piece over the centuries. The Longplayer project can also be heard online at longplayer.org.

ON THE OTHER BANK
Quantum Cloud
page 114

THAMES BARRIER

Lower Lee Crossing Roundabout – The Thames Barrier 2,450m

There is no riverside path from Bow Creek to the Thames Barrier. The land immediately adjacent to the river is split between industrial estates, derelict land and waste management sites (with some using the Thames to carry refuse away). However, there is a more interesting route that takes in the historic docks, which, once redundant, have now been redeveloped.

Royal Victoria DLR ⊖

Below: Emirates Royal Docks, the Emirates Air Line to the O₂ Arena.

SS Robin

The restored SS *Robin* is located in the Royal Victoria Dock on a pontoon. Built in 1890 at the nearby Thames Ironworks Shipyard, she is the world's oldest complete steam coaster. She plied the seas of the UK and Europe carrying grain, coal, iron, railway lines, granite blocks and barrelled herrings. She now serves as a museum, educational space and arts venue.

Tidal Basin Road

• Lower Lee
Crossing
Roundabout

Royal Victoria Dock

This dock formed one of three interconnecting 'royal' docks. Opening in 1855 in response to the ever-increasing demand by industry to convey goods into and out of London more quickly and efficiently and to accommodate the new larger steamships. With the Royal Albert Docks (1880) and King George V Docks (1921) it formed over 100 hectares of water and was the largest enclosed quay in the world, able to handle a far greater tonnage than all the other London docks. It survived longer than any other London port as it was quicker to respond to the advent of electricity and refrigeration.

The docks were badly damaged by bombing raids during the Second World War but following the war they revived and for a brief time they handled

Industrial waste transfer point for reprocessing plants further downstream.

containerised shipping. By the 1970s the Thames was too shallow for the supertankers and the docks finally fell into decline. The Royal Docks came under the control of the London Docklands Development Corporation, which oversaw the regeneration of the empty quays. Many of the warehouses were demolished to make way for new housing and retail development. Much of the north shore is now dominated by the ExCeL Exhibition Centre. Part of George V Dock was filled in to create the London City Airport.

The Lyle's Golden Syrup Tin

A large, 4m high tin of Golden Syrup is 'stuck' to the corner of the Plaistow Wharf sugar factory in Silvertown. The best view of this is from the elevated DLR platform at West Silvertown *(right)*. ⊖ The factory produces one million (smaller) tins of golden syrup every month.

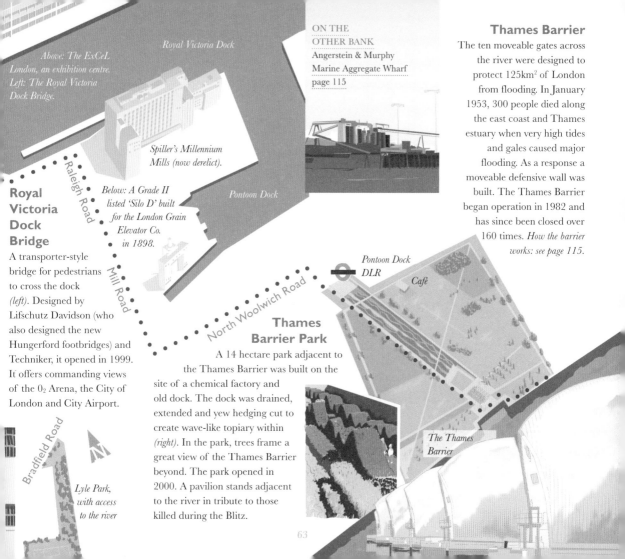

Above: The ExCeL London, an exhibition centre.
Left: The Royal Victoria Dock Bridge.

Royal Victoria Dock

Spiller's Millennium Mills (now derelict).

ON THE OTHER BANK
Angerstein & Murphy Marine Aggregate Wharf page 115

Pontoon Dock

Thames Barrier

The ten moveable gates across the river were designed to protect 125km^2 of London from flooding. In January 1953, 300 people died along the east coast and Thames estuary when very high tides and gales caused major flooding. As a response a moveable defensive wall was built. The Thames Barrier began operation in 1982 and has since been closed over 160 times. *How the barrier works: see page 115.*

Raleigh Road

Below: A Grade II listed 'Silo D' built for the London Grain Elevator Co. in 1898.

Royal Victoria Dock Bridge

A transporter-style bridge for pedestrians to cross the dock *(left)*. Designed by Lifschutz Davidson (who also designed the new Hungerford footbridges) and Techniker, it opened in 1999. It offers commanding views of the 0$_2$ Arena, the City of London and City Airport.

Mill Road

Pontoon Dock DLR

Café

North Woolwich Road

Thames Barrier Park

A 14 hectare park adjacent to the Thames Barrier was built on the site of a chemical factory and old dock. The dock was drained, extended and yew hedging cut to create wave-like topiary within *(right)*. In the park, trees frame a great view of the Thames Barrier beyond. The park opened in 2000. A pavilion stands adjacent to the river in tribute to those killed during the Blitz.

The Thames Barrier

Bradfield Road

Lyle Park, with access to the river

THE SOUTH SHORE:
A prelude

The south shore of the London Thames Path described by this book covers a distance of just over 31km (19¼ miles). Historically, the land to the south of the London Thames has been less populous than the land to north. Until about 150 years ago large sections of this area were marshlands and tidal flood plains. The slightly higher lands formed islands in the Thames. Their names still exist, such as Bermondsey, formerly Beormund Eye (or Island) and Battersea, formerly Batrichsey. One of the earliest known London settlements has been discovered on the shore at Vauxhall, it dates back to the Bronze Age (*c*.1500 BC).

To the west, towards Putney, market gardens flourished on fertile higher ground. Two hundred years ago all of this was countryside. And it was home to the few Londoners who could afford to escape the fetid airs of the City and Westminster.

The various bodies that have run Greater London have always been located on the south bank. It is as if they wanted to be detached and apart from national government at Westminster. The Archbishop of Canterbury's seat of power in London, has been at Lambeth, by the riverside, for over 800 years.

The late 1960s saw the decline of the London docks and incrementally the areas of the South Bank, Bankside and

Southwark began to transform into cultural and tourist beacons. Bankside Power Station, close to Blackfriars Bridge was transformed into the Tate Modern. Shakespeare's Globe Theatre was recreated close to where the original was built. To mark the Millennium, a footbridge was strung across the Thames to link up with St Paul's Cathedral. Numerous former docks and warehouses were restructured into shopping facilities, such as Butler's Wharf and Hay's Galleria.

Further east, not far beyond Tower Bridge, the tourists evaporate and the Thames Path becomes much quieter. Walk past derelict Tudor and Victorian dockyards, nearly all razed, to former royal palaces and on to the Greenwich Peninsula, with its white-domed entertainment arena and the Thames Barrier beyond.

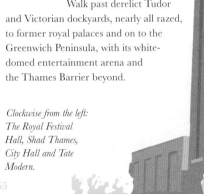

Clockwise from the left:
The Royal Festival
Hall, Shad Thames,
City Hall and Tate
Modern.

Putney Bridge

Prior to the construction of a bridge here there was a ferry crossing. In 1642, during the Civil War, a pontoon of boats was constructed to assist the Roundheads to defend London. The first bridge opened here in 1729 and was at the time only the second bridge to span the Thames in London (the other crossing was London Bridge). The original bridge had twenty-six spans, which became a hazard to shipping along the river. The present bridge *(above)* was designed by Sir Joseph Bazalgette and opened in 1886. It is 213m long and 13m wide and is the only bridge on the Thames with major churches located at each end: All Saints in Fulham *(see page 12)* and St Mary's on the southern side in Putney.

Putney Br.

St Mary's Church

Above: The Boathouse pub.

Right: Putney Railway Bridge.

Deodar Road

Wandsworth Park

St Mary's Church

There has been a place of worship on this site since the thirteenth century. This church was built in the mid-fifteenth century and was largely restructured in 1837 with the original tower being preserved. Following an arson attack in 1973, the church was restored with a contemporary interior layout. The church is renowned as the site of the Putney Debates.

The Putney Debates

In 1647 the Putney Debates took place between the representatives of Oliver Cromwell's New Model Army and civilian representatives, the Levellers, to discuss a new political constitution for England following the Civil War. These included 'one man, one vote' and constituencies to be defined by size. This was the UK's first organised political movement. Following the debates the franchise was only offered to those with property. However many of the articles discussed would appear 100 years later in the US constitution.

Putney Railway

Putney High Street

East Putney Underground

Below: The manifesto for political change, proposed by the Levellers during the English Civil War.

AN
AGREEMENT
OF THE
PEOPLE
FOR

A firme and prefent Peace, upon grounds of common-right and free-dome;

Wandsworth Park

Built on allotments and opened in 1903 by London County Council to provide recreational space for the local inhabitants, the park was also designed to break up the industrial bleakness along the south shore. The 8 hectare park is Grade II listed.

PUTNEY

Putney Bridge – Wandsworth Bridge 2,550m

The start of the Thames Path southern walk was also the starting point of English democracy. St Mary's Church, in 1647, witnessed the Putney Debates. The land then was very much countryside, but within 150 years industry had started congregate around the mouth of the River Wandle. It was a source of energy and transportation. Today the Thames is vital for the removal of waste from the borough of Wandsworth.

Wandsworth Riverside Quarter Pier

The Ship pub

Jews Row

Wandsworth Bridge

Solid Waste Transfer Station

Non-recyclable rubbish collected in the Borough of Wandsworth is taken to the waste transfer station at Smugglers Way *(left)* and Cringle Dock *(page 72)*. It is loaded into containers and transferred by barge to the electricity-from-waste incinerator at Bexley, some 34km downstream. It handles up to 5,600 tonnes of waste per week.

Wandsworth Town station

Smugglers Way

River Wandle

The Wandle rises in Croydon, some 18km to the south. By 1800 there were more than fifty water mills on this fast-flowing river, supplying power to a range of factories. Many industries grew up around the mouth of the river where it enters the Thames, producing soap, silk, gin and beer. Access to the Thames was vital for supplying raw materials to these industries and for carrying finished goods away. Young's Ram Brewery opened in 1651 and went on to become the oldest beer producer in the UK. It closed in 2006.

Surrey Iron Railway

In 1803, the Surrey Iron Railway *(right)* ran parallel to the Wandle for 13km. By the 1840s it was abandoned, as the horse-drawn trucks could no longer compete with the arrival of the steam engine.

Left: The River Wandle as it enters the Thames.

River Wandle

ON THE OTHER BANK
Hurlingham Club page 13

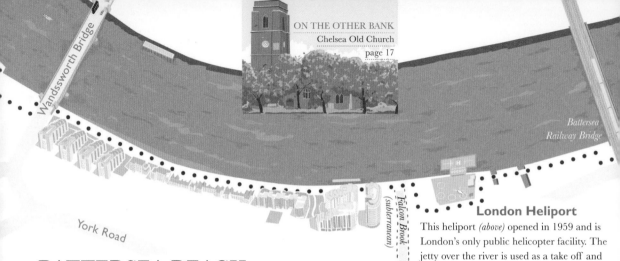

ON THE OTHER BANK
Chelsea Old Church
page 17

Battersea Railway Bridge

Wandsworth Bridge

York Road

Falcon Brook (subterranean)

London Heliport

This heliport *(above)* opened in 1959 and is London's only public helicopter facility. The jetty over the river is used as a take off and landing point.

BATTERSEA REACH

Wandsworth Bridge – Albert Bridge 2,850m

In the sixteenth century, this district was a place of retreat for many wealthy Londoners to escape the stink and turmoil of the city. Prior to the Industrial Revolution, it was awash with market gardens, which supplied fruit and vegetables to the capital. It later became home to many dissidents, including the poet and artist William Blake. The first working class person to hold a cabinet post, John Burns (1858–1943), MP for Battersea, lived here, as did the Indian-born Shapurji Saklatvala (1874–1936), one of the few communists to become an MP. A large stretch of the Thames Path along Battersea Reach is now occupied by anonymous riverside apartments built on the sites of former breweries, starch works, and candle factories.

Falcon Brook

The Falcon Brook where it entered the Thames was known as Battersea Creek. Price's Candle Factory stood on the site and used the creek as a loading dock. The creek was culverted in the 1860s and only feeds into the river, via the Falcon Brook Pumping station, when the sewage system is overloaded.

Right: St Mary's Church Battersea, with the decrepid river wall. Far right: Albion riverside. Below: a houseboat at low water.

Clapham Junction station

Grant Road

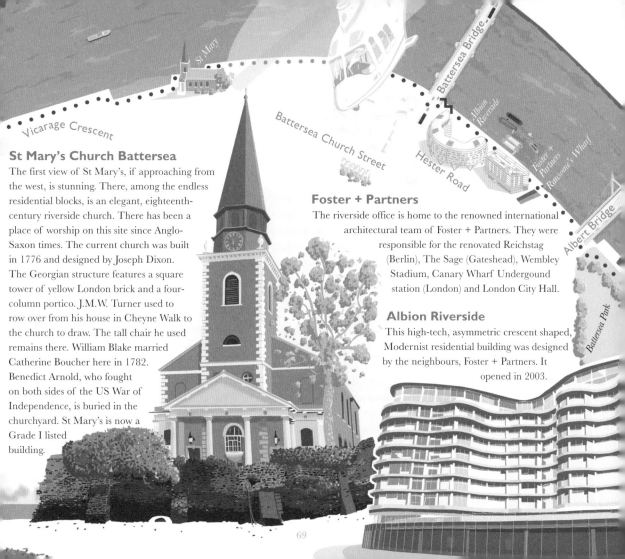

Vicarage Crescent

Battersea Church Street

Hester Road

Battersea Bridge

Albion Riverside

Foster + Partners Ransome's Wharf

Albert Bridge

Battersea Park

St Mary

St Mary's Church Battersea

The first view of St Mary's, if approaching from the west, is stunning. There, among the endless residential blocks, is an elegant, eighteenth-century riverside church. There has been a place of worship on this site since Anglo-Saxon times. The current church was built in 1776 and designed by Joseph Dixon. The Georgian structure features a square tower of yellow London brick and a four-column portico. J.M.W. Turner used to row over from his house in Cheyne Walk to the church to draw. The tall chair he used remains there. William Blake married Catherine Boucher here in 1782. Benedict Arnold, who fought on both sides of the US War of Independence, is buried in the churchyard. St Mary's is now a Grade I listed building.

Foster + Partners

The riverside office is home to the renowned international architectural team of Foster + Partners. They were responsible for the renovated Reichstag (Berlin), The Sage (Gateshead), Wembley Stadium, Canary Wharf Undergound station (London) and London City Hall.

Albion Riverside

This high-tech, asymmetric crescent shaped, Modernist residential building was designed by the neighbours, Foster + Partners. It opened in 2003.

BATTERSEA PARK

Albert Bridge – Chelsea Bridge 1,225m

Battersea Park is, at 80 hectares, the largest riverside park in London. The original site, Battersea Fields, comprised marshland and market gardens, and was noted for its asparagus and lavender.

Albert Bridge

This is probably one of the more unusual and iconic bridges across the Thames. Rowland Mason Ordish created a bridge that consisted of half suspension and half cantilevered design. It used steel rods instead of the more traditional chains and it opened in 1873, despite opposition from the operators of the nearby Battersea Bridge. Most of London's bridges were privately owned, and fees were charged to cross the river. Tolls were charged for the first six years of the Albert Bridge's life, before the Metropolitan Board of Works bought the crossing and cancelled the charges. The toll booths still remain in place. This much-loved, pastel-painted bridge has suffered over the years; its construction has not been able to withstand the rigours and motor vehicles of the twentieth century, and it has been threatened with replacement several times. Soldiers marching to or from the Chelsea Barracks were instructed to break step when crossing to prevent the constant vibration from setting up a resonance frequency that could break the bridge. A similar problem occurred when the Millennium Bridge opened in 2000 *(see page 91)*. During the latter part of the twentieth century, weight limits and a traffic 'tidal flow' system were placed on vehicles using the bridge, and a central pier was added to support the crossing. The bridge still survives and is best viewed at night, when it is illuminated with chains of lights. It has appeared as a backdrop in many films, including *A Clockwork Orange* and *Absolute Beginners*.

Albert Bridge

Albert Bridge

Albert Bridge Road

Battersea Park

Battersea Park developed out of a need for a new open space in a rapidly growing London. Spurred on by the Pimlico building developer, Thomas Cubitt, the Act of Parliament was passed in 1846. The park was raised and developed from 750,000 tonnes of earth dug from the creation of the London Docks, shipped upstream by barge. Sir James Pennethorne was commissioned to design the park. Pennethorne had previously laid out Victoria Park in the East End (opened in 1845). Both parks were created as large public spaces within the rapidly expanding urban sprawl of the metropolis. Battersea Park finally opened in 1858 by Queen Victoria, who also opened Chelsea Bridge on the same day. The bridge was a vital connection for those north of the river to access the park.

ALL TROOPS MUST BREAK STEP WHEN MARCHING OVER THIS BRIDGE

The Peace Pagoda

In 1985, on the fortieth anniversary of the atomic bombing of Hiroshima, Japanese Buddhist monks donated a peace pagoda to the park *(right)*. A four-sided statue of Buddha overlooks the Thames.

Battersea Park Children's Zoo

Battersea Fun Fair

In 1951, a pleasure garden was created as part of the Festival of Britain. The Battersea Fun Fair also opened in the same year. Though it lasted longer than the Festival, it was closed following a fatal accident in 1972, in which five children were killed on the big dipper.

Sculputres in the park include Henry Moore's Three Standing Figures *(left) and Barbara Hepworth's* Single Form.

The pumping station that was built to supply water to the lakes and waterfalls within the gardens is now the Pump House Gallery.

Boating Pond

ON THE OTHER BANK
Royal Hospital Chelsea
page 18

Chelsea Bridge

FA Rules

The first football match to be played under Football Association rules took place in the park in 1864. The park became home to the Wanderers FC who in 1872 became the first winners of the FA Cup.

Queenstown Road

N

Prince of Wales Drive

D G E M

During both World Wars anti-aircraft guns were installed to protect the capital against bombing raids.

Battersea Power Station

The initial designs for the Battersea Power Station in the 1920s were criticised as being too ugly for a structure within the capital. Sir Giles Gilbert Scott was brought in to reconsider the external fabric design of the building. The coal-fired power station went online in 1933 and was, until the 1950s, the largest power station in the UK. Every year, 1,000,000 tonnes of coal were brought upstream on low-profile boats that could get under the bridges to the purpose built dock, to feed the generators furnaces.

In 1953, the Art Deco-styled power station was expanded and a second generator added, making it the largest brick-built structure in Europe. The original Power Station A control room had been fitted out with marble and parquet flooring. Station B, however, being post-War, was not so well specified. The addition of two further 103m chimneys gave the building the symmetry we see today. At its capacity the station could generate 503 Megawatts of power. A fire within the power station in 1964 caused a power failure that delayed the launch of BBC Two by one day. Gilbert Scott would go on to design the power station further downstream at Bankside (see page 90).

By 1983 the station ceased to generate electricity and the site was sold. There has been much speculation surrounding the various plans for converting the listed structure and surrounding land. Spiralling costs of proposals and economic slumps have resulted in the land changing ownership several times since the 1980s. Work is now underway to create retail, residential and public spaces. The Thames Path will run riverside, in front of the former electricity station, once work is complete. An extension of the Northern line Underground is proposed to run from Kennington to Nine Elms and Battersea.

The former Battersea Power Station as viewed from the river

Battersea Park

Queenstown Road

Prince of Wales Drive

Battersea Park station

Battersea Dogs & Cats Home

The rescue centre, founded in 1860, moved here in 1871.

Battersea Park Road

Cringle Dock Transfer Station

This is the second transfer station (above right) in the borough of Wandsworth (see page 67). It can dispatch up to 5,000 tonnes of containerised waste per week by river to the 'Energy from Waste' centre at Belvedere in Bexley.

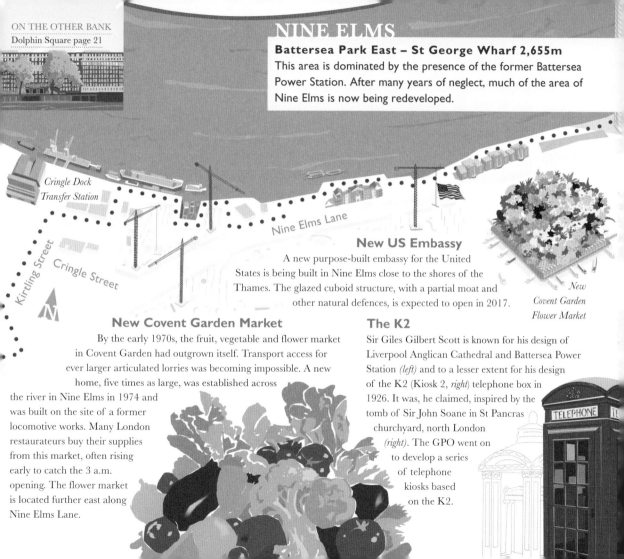

ON THE OTHER BANK
Dolphin Square page 21

NINE ELMS

Battersea Park East – St George Wharf 2,655m

This area is dominated by the presence of the former Battersea Power Station. After many years of neglect, much of the area of Nine Elms is now being redeveloped.

Cringle Dock Transfer Station

Nine Elms Lane

Kirting Street

Cringle Street

New US Embassy

A new purpose-built embassy for the United States is being built in Nine Elms close to the shores of the Thames. The glazed cuboid structure, with a partial moat and other natural defences, is expected to open in 2017.

New Covent Garden Flower Market

New Covent Garden Market

By the early 1970s, the fruit, vegetable and flower market in Covent Garden had outgrown itself. Transport access for ever larger articulated lorries was becoming impossible. A new home, five times as large, was established across the river in Nine Elms in 1974 and was built on the site of a former locomotive works. Many London restaurateurs buy their supplies from this market, often rising early to catch the 3 a.m. opening. The flower market is located further east along Nine Elms Lane.

The K2

Sir Giles Gilbert Scott is known for his design of Liverpool Anglican Cathedral and Battersea Power Station *(left)* and to a lesser extent for his design of the K2 (Kiosk 2, *right*) telephone box in 1926. It was, he claimed, inspired by the tomb of Sir John Soane in St Pancras churchyard, north London *(right)*. The GPO went on to develop a series of telephone kiosks based on the K2.

TELEPHONE

Vauxhall Bridge

The original Vauxhall crossing was the first cast-iron bridge over the Thames. It opened in 1816 and was initially called Regent Bridge, after the then Prince Regent, but was soon renamed Vauxhall Bridge. It became a popular pedestrian crossing with those accessing the Vauxhall Pleasure Gardens *(see page 76)*. The owners had hoped that the bridge would engender prosperity on the Vauxhall side and that traffic and tolls would increase. However, factories such as Doulton & Watts sprang up and the profits only ever came from the Pleasure Garden footfall.

As with most other London bridges, Vauxhall Bridge was bought by the Metropolitan Board of Works and the tolls were removed. By the late nineteenth century the bridge was under strain as it was not wide enough to cope with the increase in traffic, and the piers were eroding. A temporary crossing was installed in 1898 and Sir Alexander Binnie was commissioned to design a wider replacement. The new bridge was nearly 25m wide with five steel arches spanning the Thames. Each granite pier has a bronze statue to represent aspects of work and progress: the downstream figures are Fine Arts, Local Government, Science and Education, whilst upstream are Pottery, Engineering, Architecture and Agriculture. The new bridge, when it opened in 1906, was the first to carry trams over the Thames.

Bronze Age Pier

At extreme low tides, two rows of wooden posts can be viewed *(below right)*. They are believed to be the remains of a Bronze Age jetty (*c.*1500 BC) that ran into the river. Prior to the nineteenth-century embankment, the river was much shallower than it is today. It is believed that the jetty was used for ceremonial or funereal purposes, connecting the shore to an island within the river.

VAUXHALL

St George Wharf – MI6 Building 475m

From ancient secrets to modern spies: within several hundred metres of each other are the remains of a Bronze Age pier and the ziggurat-like home to MI6, the UK's secret service. Most of the shoreline of this section is festooned with Post-modernist architecture.

ON THE OTHER BANK
Tyburn Sluice Gate page 22

Left: The River Effra storm gate, north of Vauxhall Bridge. Below: The MI6 building.

River Effra

The River Effra rises at Crystal Palace, 14km to the south. Over the past 200 years it has been built over and culverted and is now largely a subterranean stream. In the nineteenth century, the river became part of Sir Joseph Bazalgette's sewage network. The river splits before it enters the Thames north and south of Vauxhall Bridge. The storm sluice gate below the MI6 building *(right)* marks the newer of the two exit points.

St George
Wharf Pier

Secret Intelligence Service (MI6) Headquarters

In the late 1980s, an abandoned riverside site, formerly a distillery north of Vauxhall Bridge, was purchased and the architectural practice of Terry Farrell appointed to design a complex of offices, housing, shops and a public space. The plans were rejected and the Government bought the site as a home for MI6. Farrell dramatically upgraded the security and infrastructure for the requirements of British Secret Service. The building has the appearance of a fortified Art Deco ziggurat. It opened in 1995 and has featured in several James Bond films, including *The World is not Enough* and *Skyfall*.

St George Wharf

This series of expensive glass-clad riverside apartments and a forty-eight-storey tower (181m) covers nearly 3 hectares and includes offices, retail units and restaurants. It is distinguished by its five gull-wing roofs.

Wandsworth Rd

ALBERT EMBANKMENT

MI6 Building – Lambeth Bridge 770m

A thirteenth-century mercenary's manor house would give a corruption of its name not only to this area but also to Russian railway stations and a brand of motor vehicles. The riverfront here, between 1815 and 1956, was dominated by the famous potteries of Doulton & Watt, later to become Royal Doulton.

ON THE OTHER BANK
Tate Britain
page 23

Albert Embankment

This embankment, from Vauxhall Bridge to Westminster Bridge, was built between 1866 and 1869. It was created as part of the Bazalgette London sewage project *(see pages 30–31)* and was a flood defence wall to protect Vauxhall. The shoreline was moved further into the Thames.

One of the Lion heads that decorate the Albert Embankment.

Vauxhall Pleasure Gardens

The first pleasure gardens in Vauxhall opened to the public just before the Restoration in 1660, two years after the death of the Lord Protector, Oliver Cromwell. Known originally as the New Spring Gardens, they offered elegant gardens, illuminated footpaths and fountains, hot air balloon rides and trapeze artists, plus dancing and music. It became known as a place of cultured entertainment for those who could afford the price of admission. Access from the north shore was only by ferry until Westminster Bridge was constructed in 1750. Handel's *Music for the Royal Fireworks* was premiered here in 1749 as a celebration of the end of the Austrian War of Succession a year earlier, and over 12,000 tickets were sold. Despite a profitable success for over 150 years, Vauxhall Gardens, like many other pleasure gardens *(see Cremorne Gardens page 16)* became known as an area for vice. Charles Dickens was very underwhelmed with the gardens. In *Sketches by Boz* (1836), he wrote '. . . the entrance, if there had been any magic about it at all, was now decidedly disenchanted, being, in fact, nothing more nor less than a combination of very roughly-painted boards and sawdust'. The owners went bankrupt in 1840. The operation changed hands a year later but finally closed in 1859. Workers' houses were built on the gardens shortly afterwards. By the 1940s these had become bomb-damaged slum dwellings. Lambeth Council cleared the area and restored it as a park known as Spring Gardens. It was a mere shadow of it former glory. The local community have, over recent years, attempted to inject some spirit back into the Pleasure Gardens with concerts, open-air film screenings and community events.

Left: A Vauxhall Pleasure Gardens handbill. Right: A hot air balloon, a star attraction of the gardens.

VAUXHALL GARDENS,
NOTICE!
The Lessee has the satisfaction to announce that the most signal success has crowned the Reduction of the Price of Admission to
TWO SHILLINGS
INCREASED NOVELTIES.
Vocal and Instrumental Concert
LION KING,
VAN AMBURGH
OF ANIMALS.

Water Music

On 17 July 1717, King George I, along with an entourage, were carried along the Thames from Whitehall to Chelsea whilst Handel's new composition *Water Music* was played on an accompanying barge, with an orchestra of fifty players.

Lambeth Bridge

Albert Embankment

Black Prince Road

Clockwise from the right: Lambeth Bridge, a former Vauxhall Motor insignia, pineapple capitals on Lambeth Bridge, a Russian railway sign, the former Royal Doulton factory offices in Lambeth and a Doulton logo.

Lambeth Bridge

Originally this was the site of a coach and horse ferry service. The first bridge at this location was a low-level suspension crossing designed by Peter William Barlow. It opened in 1862 but rapidly fell into disrepair. By 1910, motor vehicles were banned from using it. A new bridge was eventually commissioned and opened in 1932. The sculpted pineapples that top the pair of obelisks at the ends of the bridge are a tribute to John Tradescant the Younger, who is buried nearby at St Mary, Lambeth *(see page 78).*

Royal Doulton

The former high Victorian Gothic offices of Royal Doulton, on Black Prince Road, are all that remain of the vast ceramic factory that dominated the riverfront in Vauxhall. They used the river to carry raw materials in and finished goods out. Doulton created many building façades in London, including The Savoy, Harrods and Hay's Wharf. Clean air regulations forced the factory to move to Staffordshire in 1956.

DOULTON 1875 LAMBETH

From Falkes to Vokzal

In the thirteenth century, Sir Falkes de Breaute, a high-ranking Anglo-Norman mercenary and supporter of King John and Henry III, gained, through marriage, the estate of the Redvers family in south Lambeth. The manor house then became known as Falkes' Hall. Over time, this corrupted to Fox Hall and eventually Vaux Hall. The de Breaute coat of arms included a griffin. In the 1780s, Michael Maddox, an English theatre manager, created a pleasure garden in St Petersburg. This was known in Russian as *vokzal*, after the Vauxhall Pleasure Garden. In 1837, a railway line was built to the pleasure garden and the station was named Vokzal. This then became the generic term for Russian railway stations. Coincidentally, in 1840, a delegation arrived from Russia to study the new UK railway system. One of the stations they visited was the newly built terminus* at Nine Elms, called Vauxhall. At around the same time a marine engineering company was established in Vauxhall. By 1897 it became known as the Vauxhall Iron Works and began manufacturing motor cars. The company, to be later known as Vauxhall Motors, took the de Breaute griffin as its logo.

* The London terminus for this line would, in 1848, be moved to Waterloo.

ВОКЗАЛ

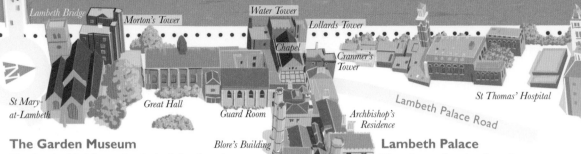

Lambeth Bridge · Morton's Tower · Water Tower · Lollards Tower · Chapel · Cranmer's Tower · St Mary-at-Lambeth · Great Hall · Guard Room · Blore's Building · Archbishop's Residence · Lambeth Palace Road · St Thomas' Hospital

The Garden Museum

The church of St Mary-at-Lambeth, dating from the 1370s, was deconsecrated in 1972 and was transformed by the Tradescant Trust into the Museum of Garden History in 1977. John Tradescant the Elder (*c*.1570–1638) was a traveller, botanist, plant hunter and gardener to the seventeenth-century English monarchy. He lived in south Lambeth. His son, also called John, followed in his father's footsteps, introducing the magnolia to the UK and cultivating the first pineapple here. After Tradescant the Younger's death, the gardens and collections were taken over by Elias Ashmole and would go on to form part of the Ashmolean Museum in Oxford. The knot garden within the church grounds dates from the time of the Tradescants. Within the churchyard are the tombs of John Tradescant the Elder and Younger. The grave of Captain Bligh of the HMS *Bounty* is also located here.

Lambeth Palace

The palace and gardens have, for over 800 years, been the London home of the Archbishops of Canterbury. In the 1190s the manor house was acquired by Archbishop Baldwin so that he could be close to the seat of power across the river at Westminster. This slightly raised piece of land may have been the site of Roman occupation. The grounds are a complex of buildings from almost every era since the twelfth century. John Wycliffe, the first person to translate the Bible into English, was imprisoned above the west end of the chapel in Lollards Tower in 1378 and tried for heresy. The gatehouse was commissioned in 1485 by Cardinal John Morton and is the oldest brick structure in London. The red-brick Gothic Great Hall contains the records of the Church of England dating as far back as the ninth century. In 1544, the Book of Common prayer was written by Archbishop Cranmer in the tower that would be later named after him. The numerous buildings of Lambeth Palace were damaged several times during the English Civil War and the Blitz, although much has been restored or replaced.

Left: St Mary-at-Lambeth. Right: Morton's Tower.

LAMBETH PALACE

Lambeth Bridge – Westminster Bridge 720m

Once this riverside stretch of the Thames was all marshland. A section of raised land became the London riverside home of the Archbishop of Canterbury in the twelfth century and more recently, St Thomas' Hospital.

Florence Nightingale Museum

St Thomas' Hospital

This hospital was built on land reclaimed following the creation of the Albert Embankment. The original hospital, named after St Thomas à Becket and founded after his canonisation in 1173, is the second oldest in London. The establishment was later rededicated to another St Thomas (the Apostle). The institution was located at Borough High Street in Southwark but was forced to move and make way for the South East Railway in 1863. The new hospital, designed by Henry Currey in an Italianate style, was influenced by the principles of open, wide wards, as advocated by the renowned nurse of the period, Florence

Left: Florence Nightingale

Nightingale. The six Nightingale blocks and the chapel were opened by Queen Victoria in 1871. Following bomb damage during Second World War only three of the pavilions survived. The replacement hospital was opened in 1976. This new thirteen-storey cuboid structure sits uncomfortably next to the original buildings. By tradition, any commoner who dies in the Palace of Westminster across the river has the location of their death marked as St Thomas' Hospital, thus eliminating the royal protocol of convening a jury of Royal household members.

Among These Dark Satanic Mills

During the 1790s the Romantic poet and artist, William Blake (1757–1827) *(right)* lived close to the Thames in the then-impoverished and noisome Lambeth Marsh. The district was heavily industrialised, with boat-building, tanneries, furnaces, potteries, mills and steam engines running around the clock. It was to this landscape that he referred, in his preface to the illustrated poem *Milton* (1804–10), as 'Among these dark Satanic Mills', a metaphor for the orthodox church. In 1916, Sir Hubert Parry set these words to music to form the famous hymn 'Jerusalem'. Blake spent his later life by the Strand and close to the Thames, which he referred to as 'like a bar of gold'.

ON THE
OTHER BANK
The Houses of
Parliament
page 24

THE WATERMEN

Before 1729 London had just one bridge across the river. The only other way to move people and goods between the two shores was by boat.

The Apprenticeship

Prior to the advent of steam power, watermen and their 'wherries' provided a vital part of the transport within London, carrying both people and goods from shore to shore. A wherry was a small clinker-built wooden boat, approximately 6.5m long and propelled by oars, which could carry up to five people. This type of vessel was ideal for reaching in over the marshlands of the east and south and the still-uncovered tributaries.

An Act of Parliament was passed in 1555 to ensure the training and regulating of the watermen's rates and the quality of service. Overcharging was a common occurrence and the reputation of the oarsmen was poor.

An apprentice waterman, often the son of a serving waterman, would serve an apprenticeship lasting seven years.

Once qualified, each waterman had his own licence number in the form of a large silver or metal badge, known as a brassard, worn on the left sleeve of his tunic, similar to the badge worn by London black cab drivers today.

The Water Taxi

Operating from 'stairs' – simple stone steps down to the river, often adjacent to a tavern or landmark – watermen would ply for business. In central London, much of this business was carrying people to and from work, theatres, pleasure gardens and other entertainments offered on the south shore.

The work of the watermen, operating in all weathers, with a tidal river, was often dangerous. The Thames was a much busier place than it is today. Passing under the narrow openings of the Old London Bridge could be a white-water experience. Many passengers preferred to disembark upstream and walk past the bridge. The Old London Bridge, acting as a weir, was partially the cause

of the river often freezing up in winter. This seriously effected the watermen's trade, as customers could simple walk over the Thames. During part of the seventeenth century they were not permitted to operate on a Sunday.

The number of watermen on the river peaked in the early eighteenth century as the population of the capital grew and before new bridges and new forms of transport arrived. However, from 1750 onwards the watermen's livelihoods became affected by the construction of more bridges across the river. Even though the new bridges charged tolls, people still preferred to pay rather than risking the water crossings.

The Decline

The advances of the Industrial Revolution and steam power saw the arrival of powered boats capable of carrying more people faster along the Thames. In 1815, the watermen took legal action to prevent the owners of the first steam package plying from Wapping Old Stairs and

Gravesend. It was akin to attempting to stop the tide; the case failed. The embankment of the river in the late nineteenth century saw the removal of stairs and sloping banks to the river, which were replaced with piers.

Royal Watermen

Monarchs had their own liveried watermen to row the royal entourage up and down the Thames from palace to palace: Greenwich, Whitehall, Hampton Court and Windsor. Today, the monarchy has a bargemaster, plus twenty-four watermen in scarlet regalia, retained for ceremonial occasions such as the opening of Parliament. They are paid an annual salary of £3.50.

The Worshipful Company of Watermen and Lightermen is a City Guild that licenses Thames watermen. It still exists today as a lobbying group that often questions and opposes the building of new bridges across the river. It also does much charitable work. Those remaining watermen still work the river on pleasure and commuter boats.

Doggett's Coat and Badge Race

Watermen often raced each other, to settle a dispute or simply to see who could reach a given point the quickest. But rarely was anything ever organised. In 1715, a rowing event began in the Thames that has taken place every year since. This little-known race has become the oldest continuous sporting event in the world. It was founded by Thomas Doggett, an Irish-born actor and theatre manager, either to celebrate the accession of the House of Hanover or to reward a waterman for getting him across the river under difficult circumstances. The race is between six watermen in their first year out of apprenticeship, over a distance of 8km (4 miles, 7 furlongs), between the piers of Old Swan *(see page 39)* at London Bridge and Cadogan in Chelsea. Doggett left an endowment that would enable the race to be contested every year in perpetuity by the Worshipful Company of Fishmongers. The winner still receives a scarlet tunic and a large silver arm badge as a prize. In 1947, nine races were held, one for each year that was missed during the Second World War. Today the watermen race in sleek fibreglass sculls, covering the course in less than 30 minutes with the tide, in huge contrast to the heavy wooden wherries rowed by their forebears, which took two hours against the tide.

Right: The scarlet uniform, including the silver medal, of the Doggett Coat and Badge winner.

The Former County Hall

In 1888, the London County Council was created to form a new metropolitan authority to govern the rapidly expanding capital. New offices and a meeting complex were required, so space previously occupied by factories and wharves was acquired across the river from Parliament and the architect Ralph Knott was appointed. He created a six-storey river-facing façade over 210m wide, with a grand concaved colonnade.

Work started in 1910 but the outbreak of the First World War delayed its completion until 1922. Various additional offices were added over the years up until the 1970s. In 1965 the LCC was reformed into a new body: the Greater London Council. In 1986 the GLC was disbanded by the Conservative government of the time, not before the Labour-controlled GLC had displayed London's unemployment figures large across the front of the building, in full view of Parliament. The County Hall offices were sold off and are now occupied by a gallery, an aquarium and two hotels and is a major London tourist hotspot.

The GLC was reborn in 2000 as the Greater London Authority. Its new home is located on the riverside opposite the Tower of London (see page 96).

County Hall, viewed from Westminster Bridge

The Guardian of Westminster Bridge

The Coade stone lion that guards the eastern end of Westminster Bridge was created originally for the Lion Brewery, Lambeth that stood where the Royal Festival Hall is now located. The lion was placed here in 1966. The factory that manufactured the artificial Coade stone (Lithodipyra) was located where County Hall is now.

LONDON EYE

Westminster Bridge – Hungerford Bridge 540m

This stretch of the river is dominated by the revolving observation platform, the London Eye, which has, in a very short space of time, become an iconic feature of the London skyline and is now probably as well known as Big Ben and Buckingham Palace.

The London Eye

The giant Ferris wheel that sits over the Thames was intended to be only a temporary structure. Originally known as the Millennium Wheel, it was conceived by the architectural firm Marks Barfield to celebrate the year 2000. Sections of the wheel were floated up the Thames on barges, assembled horizontally on piles, then raised into position. The wheel is held in place by a single cantilevered A-frame, and at 135m it is the tallest Ferris wheel in Europe. The thirty-two observation pods rotate once every 30 minutes, offering visitors tremendous views out over London and beyond. Despite the transient plans for the wheel, it has become a permanent feature of the London skyline and has carried well over 50 million passengers.

London Eye Pier

Right: The Shell Centre.

Right: Hungerford Bridge.

Jubilee Gardens

The land between the Shell Centre and the Thames is protected by a covenant, established by Shell, that prohibits any building work upon it. The land was previously used for the 1951 Festival of Britain, when it housed the Dome of Discovery. In 1977, the gardens were landscaped to commemorate the Silver Jubilee of Elizabeth II. Also located here is a memorial to the International Brigade who fought in the Spanish Civil War.

The Shell Centre

The Shell Centre is a major international office for the petroleum company Shell. It was designed by Sir Howard Robertson, who was a consultant on the design of the United Nations building in New York. Work began in 1961 on what was the site of the Festival of Britain. The twenty-seven-storey, Portland stone-clad, structure is 107m high and is made up of two complexes that straddle the railway line. Plans have been proposed to redevelop parts of the centre to incorporate residential and shopping facilities.

Festival Pier

Hungerford Bridge – Waterloo Bridge 265m

On this stretch of the Thames there once stood a gaggle of riverside manufacturing plants. Damaged by war and neglect, the land was cleared after the Second World War and was briefly home to the Festival of Britain. It is now a thriving national arts and cultural centre.

Left: Hungerford Bridge.

Right: The Festival of Britain logo.
Below left: The Royal Festival Hall.

ROYAL FESTIVAL HALL

195

The Royal Festival Hall

The Royal Festival Hall, a Grade I listed building, is a concert, dance and spoken word venue, and the only remaining structure from the Festival of Britain. The wood-panelled concert hall contains 2,500 seats and at its time of construction was considered quite radical, with much detail given to acoustics and layout, though these have been amended over the years. A notable feature is the private boxes that appear like a pulled-out drawers. Beyond the auditorium, the staircases, bars and restaurants are large and open spaces, some spilling out onto terraces, and the main entrance is via the large glass façade overlooking the Thames.

The Festival of Britain

The Festival of Britain was a collection of temporary exhibitions across the UK covering the arts and architecture, science, technology and industrial design. It was opened in 1951, as the centenary of the Great Exhibition, and as a boost the UK's morale and economy: 'a tonic for the nation'. Nearly all the pre-war industrial structures and houses were demolished to make way for the 11 hectare Festival site. The only remnant of the past was a shot tower, which was used as a radio beacon. The tallest feature was the futuristic Skylon sculpture, a symbol of the Festival's modern, forward-looking Britain. 8.5 million people visited the exhibition before it was closed in 1952. Over the next thirty years, the site would be developed as a national cultural centre known as the South Bank.

ON THE OTHER BANK
The Savoy Hotel page 33

The Undercroft

A 'clack, clack' noise alerts walkers along this part of the Thames Path that they are near to the skateboard park, a covered space beneath the Queen Elizabeth Hall. It has been a free space used by skateboarders and graffiti artists for around forty years and is very much a integral part of the South Bank sphere, despite being regularly threatened with redevelopment.

Below: The Queen Elizabeth Hall and Purcell Room with 'A Room for London' – a single-room hotel – perched on top.

Queen Elizabeth Hall and Purcell Room

Left: The Skylon, an iconic symbol of the Festival of Britain (no longer standing).

Opening in 1967, both these venues are primarily for music-based events, with 900 and 370 seats respectively and a shared foyer. The building is a bleak, squat structure, constructed in the Brutalist style of rough, exposed concrete both externally and within. Much stained by the weather, it is, undoubtedly, one of London's more controversial structures. The foyer, with a lack of windows, is very dark. Some of the external stairwells have been painted in primary colours in an attempt to 'lift' the area.

Waterloo Bridge

The first incarnation of this bridge was a nine-span crossing designed by John Rennie, which opened in 1817 as a toll bridge. Before this time there were no other Thames crossings between London and Westminster Bridges. As these two bridges were toll free, people tended to avoid Waterloo Bridge and the bridge didn't become profitable until Waterloo station opened in 1848. Originally, it was to have been called the Strand Bridge, but it was renamed following the Battle of Waterloo. When the Old London Bridge *(see page 94)* was demolished, the tidal flow became much greater and this action caused some of the piers to erode. In 1924, the bridge had to be closed completely while repairs took place. Plans and funding were sought for a replacement bridge. The second bridge, designed by Sir Giles Gilbert Scott, was opened in 1944. It was nicknamed the 'Ladies Bridge' as it was constructed mainly by women during the War owing to the lack of male labourers. It is the longest London crossing and because of its position on a bend in the Thames offers great views of London in both directions along the river towards Parliament to the south and the City to the east.

Waterloo Bridge

Waterloo Bridge

85

The National Theatre (left) and the IBM Client Centre (below), both designed by Sir Denys Lasdun. Right: ITV's London Studios

Gabriel's Wharf

Waterloo Br.

The British Film Institute

The British Film Institute (BFI), located under the southern arches of Waterloo Bridge, was founded in 1933 and is a charitable organisation that promotes and develops film production. It contains the world's largest film archive.

The Royal National Theatre

The theatre on the South Bank, the permanent home of the National Theatre, is a collection of three spaces primarily used for the production of drama and the spoken word. The foundation stone of the theatre was laid by the late Queen Mother in 1951, the year of the Festival of Britain. However, because of financial problems no further development occurred for twelve years. In 1963, Sir Denys Lasdun was appointed as the architect to the project and building work started six years later. The rough-cast concrete mirrors that of the Queen Elizabeth Hall, though the overall appearance of the structure is far more pleasing with strong horizontal and vertical geometric interlocking shapes. It opened in 1976 and comprises of three theatres: the Olivier, the Cottesloe (now the Dorfman) and the Lyttelton. The theatre received its 'royal' status in 1988, despite Prince Charles describing it as 'a clever way of building a nuclear power station in the middle of London without anyone objecting'.

London Studios

The studios and production offices of London Weekend Television opened here in 1972. The twenty-two-storey building was known then as the South Bank Television Centre. The remit of LWT was to supply weekend television to London and the home counties from Friday evening until early Monday morning. The station merged with Carlton TV in 2002 to become ITV London, a seven-day-a-week TV operation. The building is now called the London Studios and is also home to an ITV production company responsible for many popular programmes.

NATIONAL FILM THEATRE

NATIONAL THEATRE

Waterloo Bridge – Blackfriars Bridge 905m

The South Bank cultural complex extends under Waterloo Bridge and beyond with the British Film Institute and the National Theatre. Further east is another of London's instantly recognisable landmarks: the OXO Tower.

The foreshore at Bankside is accessible at low water.

Bernie Spain Gardens

Upper Ground

Blackfriars Bridge

Gabriel's Wharf

The wharf is a part of the not-for-profit Coin Street Community Builders, a co-operative established in 1984 to resist the building of yet more large office blocks and to maintain the community for local inhabitants. The CSCB, along with a housing trust, transformed a derelict 5 hectare site adjacent to the river into a neighbourhood of houses, shops, open spaces, galleries, cafés and bars that incorporated the OXO Tower complex. An area of land was cleared to make way for an open garden space and Gabriel's Wharf that backed onto the Thames. Profits generated by the scheme are reinvested back into the community.

ON THE OTHER BANK
Somerset House
page 34

Right: The OXO Tower.

OXO Tower

The building was originally a power station that supplied electricity to the Post Office. In the late 1920s, it was converted into a meat processing and storage factory for the Liebig's Extract of Meat Company. Barges were able to pass directly into the processing plant to load and unload. Their best-known product was the OXO cube. As all forms of advertising were, and still are, banned adjacent to the river, the architect Albert Moore designed a 67m tower with glazed panels that spelled out the name OXO, especially when illuminated at night. Though the building no longer has associations with OXO, the manufacturers of the stock cube still benefit from the free advertisement. The structure was saved from demolition in the 1980s and is now divided into retail, restaurant and residential units.

Blackfriars Bridge path underpass displays a history of the bridge on tile panels.

THE FROST FAIRS

In meteorological terms, the years between the sixteenth and the nineteenth centuries were referred to as the 'Little Ice Age'. During this period, the Thames in London froze over at least twenty-two times. The nineteen piers of the Old London Bridge, with its narrow arches *(see page 94)* caused the upstream river to slow down. During the colder winters in London the ice could be up to 28cm thick in places and enterprising Londoners saw a chance to make a profit from the freeze. The opening of the new London Bridge in 1831, with fewer arches and the later embankment *(see page 30)* of the Thames caused the river to flow faster and reduced the chance of freezing. The last frost fair, before the old bridge was removed, was in early 1814.

Typesetting on Ice

Visitors to the frozen river were able to take away a memento of their visit by purchasing a personalised printed ticket. These became very popular. The centre of printing in London at this time was in Fleet Street, so it did not take long for some enterprising printers to shift a letterpress and some type down on to the ice. It could be a very profitable business. The diarist John Evelyn wrote in 1684, ''twas estimated the printer gained five pound a day, for printing a line only, at six-pence a name.'

George Wheeler. Esq

Printed on the River Thames
February 4 in the 54th year of
King George IIId Anno 1814

Printed opp Queenhithe Stairs

Above: The Old London Bridge c. 1700s.

A Winter Festival

Many forms of entertainment took place on the ice, including bear-baiting, ox-roasting, food stalls and printing presses, and of course ice skating. John Evelyn wrote: 'Coaches plied from Westminster to the Temple, and from several other stairs to and fro, as in the streets; sleds, sliding with skates, a bull-baiting, horse and coach races, puppet plays and interludes, cooks, tippling and other lewd places, so that it seemed to be a bacchanalian triumph, or carnival on the water.'

Hardship

The freezing of the Thames caused much hardship. Once this major corridor of commerce became jammed with ice, many staple items such as coal and corn became scarce and prices inflated. Whilst the festival of a frozen river was a distraction for the middle classes, those who were unable to ply their trade on the river – lightermen, watermen and dockers – became unemployed. Livelihoods were lost and many workers and families went hungry. Some simply died of hypothermia.

89

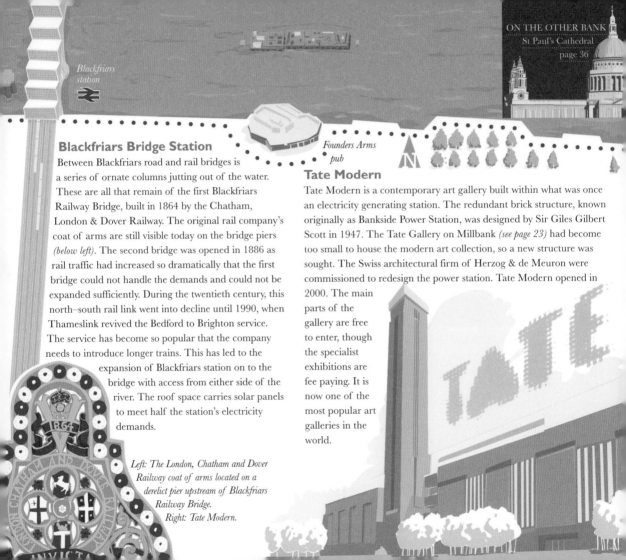

ON THE OTHER BANK
St Paul's Cathedral
page 36

Blackfriars station

Founders Arms pub

Blackfriars Bridge Station

Between Blackfriars road and rail bridges is a series of ornate columns jutting out of the water. These are all that remain of the first Blackfriars Railway Bridge, built in 1864 by the Chatham, London & Dover Railway. The original rail company's coat of arms are still visible today on the bridge piers *(below left)*. The second bridge was opened in 1886 as rail traffic had increased so dramatically that the first bridge could not handle the demands and could not be expanded sufficiently. During the twentieth century, this north–south rail link went into decline until 1990, when Thameslink revived the Bedford to Brighton service. The service has become so popular that the company needs to introduce longer trains. This has led to the expansion of Blackfriars station on to the bridge with access from either side of the river. The roof space carries solar panels to meet half the station's electricity demands.

Left: The London, Chatham and Dover Railway coat of arms located on a derelict pier upstream of Blackfriars Railway Bridge.
Right: Tate Modern.

Tate Modern

Tate Modern is a contemporary art gallery built within what was once an electricity generating station. The redundant brick structure, known originally as Bankside Power Station, was designed by Sir Giles Gilbert Scott in 1947. The Tate Gallery on Millbank *(see page 23)* had become too small to house the modern art collection, so a new structure was sought. The Swiss architectural firm of Herzog & de Meuron were commissioned to redesign the power station. Tate Modern opened in 2000. The main parts of the gallery are free to enter, though the specialist exhibitions are fee paying. It is now one of the most popular art galleries in the world.

BANKSIDE

Blackfriars Bridge Station – Southwark Bridge 660m

The return of a Shakespearean playhouse, along with the conversion of a former electricity generating station into a large contemporary, internationally renowned art gallery, has regenerated the whole area along this bank of the River Thames.

Bankside Pier

Bankside

Southwark Bridge

Millennium Footbridge

The pedestrian bridge *(above)* opened in June 2000, and was designed as a pedestrian link between Tate Modern and St Paul's Cathedral. However, it closed two days later when a serious defect arose. A lateral wobble was generated as people walked over the bridge. It instantly became known as the Wobbly Bridge. Designed by Foster + Partners, along with engineers Ove Arup and the sculptor Sir Anthony Caro. The repairs did not allow the bridge to be re-opened until 2002.

49 Bankside

It is claimed that Sir Christopher Wren lived in this house *(above)* during the construction of St Paul's Cathedral, as the north-facing windows have fantastic views of it. St Paul's was completed in 1711, around the time 49 Bankside was built, so this claim is very unlikely. In the 1950s, the owner of No. 49 removed the plaster plaque *(above)* from a nearby building that was being demolished to make way for the Bankside Power Station and mischievously stuck it on his own house.

Here Lived Sir Christopher Wren during the building of St Pauls Cathedral

Here Also in 1502 Catherine Infanta of Castile & Aragon. afterwards first Queen of King Henry VIII took shelter on her first landing in London

Shakespeare's Globe

This is a reconstruction of a the original Globe Theatre, built in 1599 on a nearby site by the Lord Chamberlain's Men, the theatrical company that included William Shakespeare *(below right)* among its members. Several of his plays were performed here. The Globe was demolished in 1644 following its closure two years earlier by the Puritans.

The concept of rebuilding the theatre was that of American actor and director Sam Wanamaker. He started the project in 1970 but never lived to see the Globe open with a performance of Shakespeare's *Henry V*. As very few original drawings survived, this is a best guess at what the first theatre looked like. Shakespeare's Globe has been rebuilt using only oak as the main structure. It is an open-air theatre built in the round. The seating areas and stage are covered with a thatch roof. The Globe is open from May to early October.

Southwark Bridge

Bank End

The Anchor

Clink Street

The Clink Prison Museum

Winchester Geese

The 28 hectares around Southwark Cathedral, wonderfully known as 'The Liberty of the Clink', had a poor reputation, as many forms of popular entertainment – such as theatres, baiting pits, gaming dens and brothels – were established here in the fifteenth and sixteenth centuries. Such activities were not permitted in the City of London. Brothels within the area had to be licensed by the Bishop of Winchester, who seemed happy to receive funds from immoral earnings. Consequently the prostitutes of the area became known as 'Winchester Geese'.

SOUTHWARK CATHEDRAL

Southwark Bridge – London Bridge 600m

Southwark has always been the poor relation of the wealthier City across the river. Much of this walk is through old, narrow, historic streets away from the Thames. The area has almost become a living museum.

The Clink Prison Museum

The Clink Prison Museum stands on the site of a medieval prison known as 'The Clink'. (The borough of Southwark, once renowned for its criminal population, had five prisons, including Marshalsea, where Charles Dickens' father was imprisoned for debt.) During the anti-Catholic Riots of 1780, The Clink prison was attacked, the prisoners released and the jail razed. It was never rebuilt. The prison's name 'clink' has become a generic term for any jail.

Borough Market

The first market was established here in 1014 and its proximity to the river assisted its growth. Since the 1860s the market has been literally overrun by railway tracks: its location close to London Bridge and Cannon Street stations has seen railway viaducts built over the top of the market. Despite some major structural modification, the market has continued to thrive. This is both a retail market (Wednesday–Saturday) and a wholesale market (weekdays). It has, over the past twenty years, become a very fashionable place for the public to purchase esoteric and speciality foods.

Left: The remaining west wall of Winchester Palace on Clink Street.

Clink Street

Right: Southwark Cathedral.

Montague Close

Winchester Palace

This palace was home to the Bishops of Winchester. Winchester in Hampshire is some 95km to the south-west of London and was once the Saxon capital. When London became the capital of England, the bishops needed a seat closer to the new centre of power. Bishop Henry of Blois was responsible for the construction of the palace by the Thames. The river gave the bishops safe and rapid access to Westminster and other royal palaces until the seventeenth century, when it was turned over to commercial usage before being destroyed by fire in 1814.

Cathedral Street

Montague Close

Southwark Cathedral

Compared to other London cathedrals, this is a modest structure. This place of worship was originally called St Mary Overie (meaning 'over the river'), with St Saviour tagged onto the name in 1540. It was not designated a cathedral until 1905. An Augustinian priory was founded here in the early twelfth century and a hospital was established close by. Edmund Shakespeare, brother of William, was buried here in 1607, though his grave is now unmarked. A stained-glass window is dedicated to the works of his brother. In the same year, Robert and Katherine Harvard, whose family were business associates of Shakespeare's father, produced a son, John. John was baptised in the church and, following the death of his entire family from the plague, emigrated to America in 1637. A year after he arrived, he too died, leaving his family library and estate to establish a new college in Massachusetts, to be named after himself. There is a Harvard chapel within the cathedral. Having survived the Great Fire of London, it is one of the capital's oldest Gothic churches, though it was largely rebuilt and restored in the nineteenth and twentieth centuries, renewing much of the fabric of the building. The churchyard has been reduced following expansion of the rail network and the shifting of London Bridge westward in 1831.

London Bridge

BOROUGH MARKET

Girolle
£5.20 PER 100 grm

Oyster
£1.90 PER 100 grm

OLD LONDON BRIDGE

There has been a bridge on this section of the Thames for nearly 2,000 years. The location of this crossing was one of the key factors in the establishment of the City of London.

Early Bridges

The invading Romans were the first to throw a bridge across the Thames at Southwark, in AD 52. The marching Roman legions heading up from Kent found that they could safely cross the river at this point.

At this time the river was fordable at low tide and so it was relatively straightforward to create a bridge at this stretch. Seagoing vessels could to reach this point at higher water and a supply of fresh water from the River Walbrook *(see page 38)* made this the ideal location for the invaders to secure their hold on the country. The City of London was thus created.

Over the next thousand years a series of wooden bridges were created for armies, traders and the populace to cross. It soon became an economic and military strategic keystone. In 1014, Olaf, King of Norway sailed up the Thames to assist King Ethelred and the English to overcome the Danes, who had taken control of London Bridge. Olaf's men attached cables from their boats to the bridge piers and sailed away using the power of the tide and wind to collapse the bridge. It is most likely this event that gave us the nursery rhyme 'London Bridge is Falling Down'.

The First Stone Bridge

The first permanent bridge was commissioned by Henry II. The work was overseen by the priest, Peter de Colechurch, which started in 1176 and took thirty-three years to complete. It was 276m long and 6m wide, with a drawbridge at the Southwark end to allow larger vessels through. Colechurch ensured a chapel was built on the bridge and, following his death, his body was laid to rest within it. The addition of houses and shops upon the bridge and tolls for traffic and pedestrians, ensured an income for the maintenance of the structure.

This London Bridge consisted of nineteen small arches, which acted as a weir, damming up the tidal river. It made crossing under the bridge at high water a very dangerous task. The difference in levels could be as much as 1.5m. The restrictions to the flow of water caused the Thames to freeze up during colder winters *(see page 88)*. By the 1720s, traffic became so congested on the narrow bridge that the Lord Mayor of London decreed, for the first time in the country, that all vehicles must travel the left hand side of the road. The appearance of the bridge

changed frequently as houses disintegrated and were replaced with new structures. The bridge managed to survive the Great Fire of London in 1666, though the water wheel, used for pumping water into the city, was destroyed.

By 1762, all the houses on the bridge were removed, along with several central arches, to allow large vessels to reach further upstream.

The Bridge House Estates

In 1282, after the wife of Henry III declined funds for the maintenance of London Bridge, an organisation was established by Royal Charter. Using toll money and charitable donations, the Bridge House Estates were able to build up a huge portfolio of properties. They became responsible for funding several London crossings, including Blackfriars, Tower and Southwark bridges. They also now maintain the Millennium Bridge. Surplus funds from the trust are now donated to London-related charities.

The Rennie Bridge

The old medieval bridge was well passed its life expectancy by the turn of the nineteenth century. In 1821, Scottish engineer John Rennie proposed a new London Bridge. However Rennie died later that year and his son, also called John, oversaw the construction work. It was to be built some 30m upstream of the existing bridge. This allowed the old crossing to be used up until the new bridge was ready. Several of the old pedestrian storm refuges were removed and rebuilt in Victoria Park and Guy's Hospital. Some small sections of the Rennie Bridge have also survived. A tunnel and a set of stairs are still in use on the southern end of the bridge. The stairs, known as 'Nancy's Steps' featured Charles Dickens' *Oliver Twist*. This is the location where Nancy is overheard assisting Oliver and not the location, as the plaque states, where she was murdered by her boyfriend Bill Sikes.

Above: London Bridge c.1600. Below: London Bridge c.1890. Left: The Bridge House Estates logo.

CITY HALL

London Bridge – Tower Bridge 930m

A great many pre-war warehouses and wharves have been demolished to make way for modernity. Downriver of London Bridge, only St Olaf House and Hay's Dock have survived the bulldozer.

London Bridge Pier

London Bridge

Right: St Olaf House.
Below: London Bridge.

Tooley Street

St Olaf House

This Swedish-influenced structure *(left)* was designed by Harry Stuart Goodhart-Rendel and built on the site of an old church, St Olave's. The Portland stone-clad offices, for the Hay's Wharf Company, opened in 1931. The decorative friezes, denoting commerce, were created by Frank Owen Dobson (1888–1963). Confusingly the name of the building from the river side is shown as Hay's Wharf whilst officially the building is known as St Olaf House. It is now part of the London Bridge private hospital.

Duke Street Hill

Tooley Street

London Bridge station

The New London Bridge

In 1904, London Bridge had to be widened to allow for greater road traffic. By the 1960s, demand had grown much further and a new bridge was proposed. The old Rennie bridge was sold to the McCulloch Oil Company, dismantled and was rebuilt in Lake Havasu, Arizona. The new six-lane crossing opened in 1973. The crossing has heated pavements so that they will not ice over in the winter months.

ON·THE·GROUND·OCCUPIED·BY·THIS·BUILDING STOOD·FORMERLY·THE·CHURCH·OF·ST.OLAVE·THIS CHURCH·WAS·FOUNDED·IN·THE·ELEVENTH·CENTURY IN·MEMORY·OF·ST·OLAF·OR·OLAVE·KING·OF·NORWAY WHO·IN·THE·YEAR·1014·HELPED·KING·ETHELRED DEFEND·THE·CITY·OF·LONDON·AGAINST·THE·DANES THE·ORIGINAL·BUILDING·SURVIVED·UNTIL·1734·AND WAS·THEN·REBUILT·TO·THE·DESIGNS·OF·HENRY FLITCROFT·IT·WAS·DAMAGED·BY·FIRE·IN·1843 AND·REBUILT·AFTERWARDS·TO·THE·SAME·DESIGN IT·WAS·DEMOLISHED·IN·1928·THE·PROCEEDS·OF THE·SALE·OF·THAT·PORTION·OF·THE·SITE·VESTED IN·THE·BERMONDSEY·BOROUGH·COUNCIL·HAVE BEEN·APPLIED·TO·THE·ESTABLISHMENT·OF A·RECREATION·GROUND·IN·TANNER·STREET·SE1

HMS *Belfast*

The Town-class cruiser HMS *Belfast* was built at the Harland and Wolff shipyard, Belfast, and launched in 1938. She and her 1,963 crew saw action during the Second World War with Arctic convoy protection of shipping to the Soviet Union and during the Allied D-Day landings at Gold and Juno beaches in 1944. HMS *Belfast* was later involved in the Korean War (1950–2) as a United Nations ship. In 1963 the Belfast was decommissioned and returned to Devonport. She was later moved to the Pool of London and opened on Trafalgar Day, 21 October 1971, where she is now a museum ship and part of the Imperial War Museum.

ON THE OTHER BANK
Tower of London page 44

Tower Bridge

Hay's Galleria

Hay's Dock was once a tea importing wharf where clippers could access the small off-river dock. A lock gate would maintain the water level at low tide. It was owned by the Hay's Wharf Company. In the 1980s, the wharf was redeveloped and the dock filled in and a covered roof was added whilst retaining much of the 1850s structure. It is now an elegant curved shopping arcade with offices and living spaces above. The riverside pub the 'Horniman at Hays' commemorates the tea importing past.

City Hall

This 'wonky' glass sphere, designed by Foster + Partners, has been home to the Greater London Authority (GLA), the twenty-five London Assembly members and the Mayor of London since 2002. It sits on a site cleared of wharf buildings. The building, open to the public, is strategically located to offer superb views of the Tower of London and Tower Bridge. The ground floor features an aerial map that displays 2,600km² of London. An asymmetric spiral ramp, over 500m long, accesses all ten floors of the structure and provides visitors with views into the building's interior: transparent government made a reality? The building's name is misleading, as it does not serve a city (nor the City, across the river) but the thirty-two boroughs of London.

Above: Hay's Galleria. Above right: The City Hall.
Left: A potted history inscribed onto the front of St Olaf House.

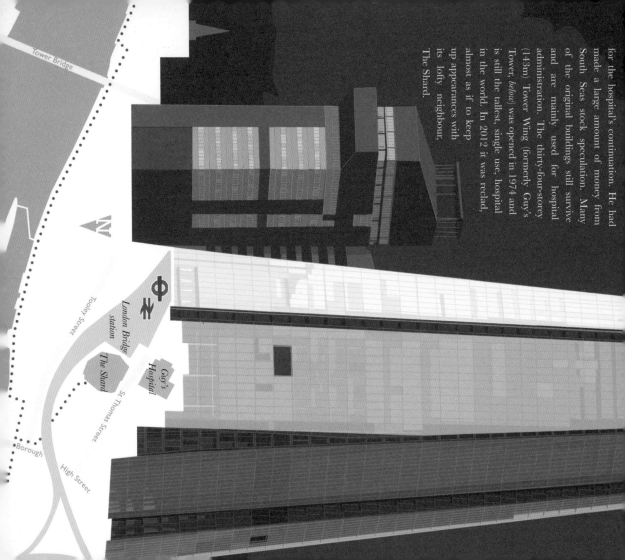

for the hospital's continuation. He had
made a large amount of money from
South Seas stock speculation. Many
of the original buildings still survive
and are mainly used for hospital
administration. The thirty-four-storey
(143m) Tower Wing (formerly Guy's
Tower, *below*) was opened in 1974 and
is still the tallest, single use, hospital
in the world. In 2012 it was reclad,
almost as if to keep
up appearances with
its lofty neighbour,
The Shard.

Tower Bridge

N

London Bridge
station

The Shard

Guy's
Hospital

Tooley Street

St Thomas Street

Borough

High Street

THE SHARD

The Shard, the tallest building in Western Europe, has become an almost instant exemplary structure on the London horizon.

Two thousand years ago, two Roman villas stood on the site of The Shard. Italian architect Renzo Piano was appointed to design a tall structure, on behalf of Sellar Property and LBQ Ltd, a Qatari investment joint venture. In 1977, Piano had created, along with Richard Rogers, the Pompidou Centre in Paris.

The design of The Shard (*right*) was inspired by paintings of ship masts in the London docks and English church spires. It was planned that the tower would offer a mixture of offices, hotels, residential, bars, shops and a viewing platform. It was described by the owners as a 'vertical slice of a city' and at 310m high (ninety-five storeys) it is the tallest building in Western Europe.

The Shard opened in 2012, at a cost of £435 million, with the public viewing platform opening a year later. On a clear day observers can see over 55km; as far as the Thames estuary. In high winds, the top of the tower can sway up to 50cm.

Its location, away from other high-rise towers, offers a singular 'spike' on the horizon. Viewed from a distance, The Shard has a lightness that many other tall structures lack. The glass façade changes it colour depending upon the time of day and weather.

The term 'The Shard' came from criticism by English Heritage, who said the building would be 'shard of glass through the heart of historic London.'

Guy's Hospital

This now NHS hospital was founded by Thomas Guy in 1721 as a place for 'incurables' that the nearby 'St Thomas' Hospital refused. Guy died three years later and left a huge endowment of £20,000

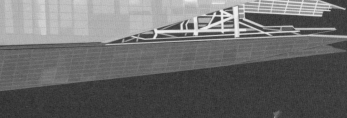

BERMONDSEY

Tower Bridge – Cherry Garden Pier 1,360m

Bermondsey was once an island surrounded by marshland. This was typical of this area, south of the Thames, before the river was embanked and the land drained. By the eighteenth century this area of south-east London was dominated by the 'stink' trades of tanning and glue manufacturing.

— Pedestrian lift

BUTLERS WHARF

Shad Thames

Butler's Wharf

These former Victorian riverside warehouses on Shad Thames, built in 1874, fortunately survived the bombs and bulldozers of the twentieth century. Butler's Wharf formed the largest wharves on the Thames in London. Some of the high-level interconnecting gangways, were used to move goods from building to building, are still visible from the pedestrianised street below. In the early 1980s the warehouses were converted into desirable flats, retail and restaurant units.

The Design Museum

This museum of contemporary design (above) opened in 1989 with the financial assistance and motivation of Sir Terence Conran. It displays frequently changing exhibitions of product, graphic, fashion and architectural design in a two-storey former banana warehouse. In 2016 the Design Museum will move to a new larger location in West London and the building will become an exhibition arena for Zaha Hadid Architects.

Left: Shad Thames.
Above: The Design Museum.
Right: St Saviour's Dock at low tide.

St Saviour's Dock

Bermondse

Subterranean River Necking

Jacob's Island

Shad Thames

Jamaica Road

100

Tower Bridge Moorings at Downings Roads

This sizeable collection of boats and barges *(below left)* on the river forms one of the oldest surviving moorings on the Thames. These ancient mooring are over 200 years old. They provide permanent living space for around a hundred people on thirty boats. Numerous Thames lighters and old working boats have been converted into garden space for growing organic fruit, vegetables and even trees, making the Tower Bridge Moorings at Downings Roads very unique on the River Thames.

ON THE OTHER BANK
St Katherine
Docks page 46

Cherry Garden Pier

Right and above: Tower Bridge Moorings.

Bermondsey Wall East

Wall West

East Lane

Chambers Street

Loftie St

River Neckinger

This river has two outlets; one here in St Saviour's Dock and the other by Gabriel's Wharf *(see page 87)*. It was both a river and a drainage dyke for the then marshy area of Bermondsey. As with all the other central London rivers, it has been culverted below the streets. In the thirteenth century, the monks of a nearby Benedictine monastery diverted the river to power a mill wheel. Later, the river became vital in the development of tanneries in this location. A water mill was also established at a gunpowder factory by the Neckinger. The mouth of the Neckinger was widened and warehouses added to accommodate merchant vessels. Many of the warehouses have survived and been converted into offices and living quarters. The word Neckinger means 'devils neckcloth', or noose. It is believed that pirates were hung close to the mouth of the river and the bodies displayed as a deterrent to others.

Jacob's Island

This was once a man-made island *(left)*, created by a loop in the River Neckinger. By the nineteenth century the poor dwellings had become notorious as one of the worst slums in the capital. Charles Dickens used this location for the home of Bill Sikes in the novel *Oliver Twist*. Dickens describes the location as 'where the buildings on the banks are dirtiest and the vessels on the river blackest with the dust of colliers and the smoke of close-built low-roofed houses, there exists the filthiest, the strangest, the most extraordinary of the many localities that are hidden in London'. Several outbreaks of cholera started on the island in the 1850s. The Great Fire of Southwark, in 1861, razed most of the slums. Today, as with most riverside locations, Jacob's Island is occupied with fine residential blocks, complete with a water feature where the River Neckinger once meandered.

◁ Gabriel's Wharf

R Thames

St Saviour's Dock ▷

ROUTE OF THE RIVER NECKINGER

DEATH AND THE THAMES

In the first chapter of *Our Mutual Friend* by Charles Dickens, Gaffer Hexam and his daughter Lizzie, are rowing over the river near Southwark Bridge, scouting for floating bodies recently deceased. In the opening sequence of Alfred Hitchcock's film *Frenzy*, the body of a young female is seen floating along the Thames. Art imitating death.

In September 2001 a headless torso was found in the Thames near Tower Bridge. It was believed to be that of a young Nigerian boy, possibly a victim of an occult practice. He was named Adam by the police. The murderer was never found. The River Thames, in art and in life, has always been connected with death.

Prior to the Bazalgette sewage reforms of the 1860s and 1870s, much of London's detritus often ended up in the river including the remains of deceased animals and murder victims. The Thames was often the place to discard or hide murdered bodies, either whole or dismembered. Heads, torsos and limbs were and are frequently washed up on the shores of the Thames, often miles away from where they were deposited. The river washes away the evidence. The Victorian press would love a mystery body found in the Thames. Nothing has really changed.

The river's dark and viscous waters have always drawn people towards it, be it for trade, pleasure or even suicide. A lighterman could fall between vessels whilst carrying a heavy load; a wherry could overturn in the powerful tides and rip currents around a bridge's stanchions spilling the passengers into the fetid waters. Death is not always accidental.

Some see the river as an 'escape' from life, awaiting a quiet moment on a bridge to jump. Suicides can be meticulously planned; waiting for dark, locating the fastest part of the river, attaching weights to their clothing, carrying money and written arrangements for their funerals.

Three of London's bridges have become infamously associated with death and suicide. As the high tide ebbed back towards the sea through the narrow arches and piers of the Old London Bridge, many passengers refused to travel with the ferryman for fear of riding the rapids, such was the force of the water. They would disembark on the western side, walk past the bridge and pick up their ferry on the eastern side. Many inexperienced ferrymen died whilst navigating the arches of the bridge. In the century before the old bridge was removed about 5,000 people died whilst 'shooting the rapids', mostly by accident.

In 1689, John Temple, son of Sir William Temple, Secretary of War, committed suicide by jumping from a ferry boat just as it entered the arches. His pockets, it was discovered later, were full of stones.

The toll on Blackfriars Bridge was removed in 1811 and the suicide rate suddenly went up. People were not going to pay a halfpenny to throw themselves in to the river.

When Waterloo Bridge opened in 1817 pedestrians were charged one penny to cross the bridge. This deterred some wishing to end their lives. However, others knew that as a consequence of the toll, the bridge would be a quiet place to jump. Once the tolls were removed in 1879 the bridge became a magnet for suicide attempts. Perhaps it was the striking last views of London that attracted them? No coincidence then that later a Royal National Lifeboat Institute boathouse was eventually located on the north shore of the bridge.

A Bulgarian exile and journalist, Georgi Markov, was stabbed by a stranger with an umbrella on the southern end of Waterloo Bridge in 1978. He died in hospital four days later of ricin poisoning. Markov had been critical of the Communist regime in his homeland and was threatened to cease his broadcasts on the BBC. It is widely believed that he was killed by a Bulgarian secret agent.

In June 1982, Roberto Calvi, chairman of Banco Ambrosiano, Italy's second largest private bank (nicknamed 'God's bank' for its connections with the Vatican) was found hanging under Blackfriars Bridge with $14,000 and five bricks in his pockets. An initial postmortem said that he had committed suicide following the bank's collapse and that he was suspected of embezzling funds. Calvi was a member of the illegal P2 masonic lodge, often referred to as 'frati neri' or 'black friars'. Was his place of death under the bridge a coincidence?

A second inquest conducted in 1983 produced an open verdict. With new evidence his family believed that Calvi had been murdered by the Mafia. Despite a lengthy investigation and trial in Italy, no one was ever charged with his murder.

On the evening of 3 September 1878, a paddle steamer, the SS *Princess Alice*, with about 750 day trippers and crew, was heading from Gravesend back towards London when she cut across the path of the seabound steam collier the *Bywell Castle* on a stretch of the river known as Gallion's Reach. The collier, though unladen, was unable to stop and smashed directly into the much smaller pleasure boat. Sliced in half, the *Princess Alice* sank within four minutes. Trapped within the boat many people drowned, and many of those who managed to swim free were overcome by the pollution in the river.

An hour prior to the collision, the recently established sewage pumping stations at Beckton and Crossness had just discharged 350,000m³ of raw sewage into the Thames on the ebb tide. Many of the initial survivors were to later die as a result of ingesting toxic waste. Approximately 600 people died in the disaster. Inventories of who boarded the *Princess Alice* were not accurate. It became the worst peacetime transport disaster in the UK. As a consequence, the laws governing inland water navigation were drastically updated, enforcing ships to pass 'port side to port side'. Six years later, the *Bywell Castle* 'vanished' whilst crossing the Bay of Biscay.

In the early hours of 20 August 1989, a pleasure boat, the *Marchioness*, carrying 132 party-goers, was hit by a dredger *Bowbelle*, as they both passed under Southwark Bridge heading east. The *Bowbelle* was 1,880 tonnes and 80m in length whilst the *Marchioness* was a mere 46 tonnes and 26m long. The pilot of the dredger was completely unaware that they had hit the pleasure cruiser and sailed on. The *Marchioness* sank within a minute, drowning fifty-one people. Despite a public inquiry no one was ever prosecuted. A memorial to the victims is located in the nave of Southwark Cathedral.

ON THE OTHER BANK
The Prospect of Whitby
page 49

Below right: Remains of King Edward III's Manor House. Below: A statue of Dr Alfred Salter.

The Leaning Tower

This now-solitary house *(left)* was once an office for a company of lightermen, who loaded and offloaded ships in the river.

King Edward III's Manor House

A series of man-made mill streams used to run down to the Thames. These were constructed to drain the marshlands. King Edward III (r.1327–77) built a manor house here, complete with a moat fed from the streams. The building later became a pottery and all that remains of the house are the foundations. Originally, the manor house stood next to the Thames, today it is some 20m inland.

King's Stairs Garden

Dr Alfred Salter

Alfred Salter was born in Greenwich in 1873. He qualified as a doctor at Guy's Hospital in 1896 and became a GP in nearby Bermondsey. He became deeply affected by the poverty and slum dwellings of his patients. With his wife Ada, he set about trying to alleviate these difficulties, with a free medical practice for those who could not afford to pay for treatment. Dr Salter felt he could make a greater impact by becoming a politician, first serving as a councillor, then in 1922, as Labour MP for Bermondsey West. In the same year, Ada Salter became the first female mayor of a London borough. A statue of Dr Salter and his daughter is located by the Thames in Cherry Garden, just above King Edward III's Manor House.

St Mary the Virgin

A place of worship has stood on this site *(above)* for over 1,000 years. This current structure was begun in 1716 to replace the twelfth-century church. The captain of the *Mayflower*, Christopher Jones, is buried in the graveyard. The *Mayflower* carried the Pilgrim Fathers to the New World in 1620. The church contains a bishop's chair made from timbers salvaged from HMS *Temeraire*, a ship made famous by a painting by J.M.W. Turner.

ROTHERHITHE

Cherry Garden Pier – Surrey Water Bridge 1,130m

By the nineteenth century, the Thames east of Tower Bridge was so packed with shipping that to build a bridge at this point became an impossibility. Crossings would have to go under the river and new tunnelling techniques acquired.

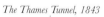

The Mayflower Pub

There has been a pub *(left)* on this site since the sixteenth century. The *Mayflower* was moored adjacent to the hostelry prior to sailing to Plymouth *en route* to the New World. The Mayflower is the only pub in the UK licensed to sell postage stamps of both the UK and the USA.

The Thames Tunnel

Rotherhithe Street

The Thames Tunnel

The growth of London in the early 1800s increased the flow of traffic over London Bridge. A need arose for a new crossing to be built further east along the river. A bridge was not practical, given the height it would have to be to allow ships through. Tunnelling was the only option but it would have to cut through the soft clay and gravel beneath the river. An initial attempt was tried in 1808 and failed. In 1825, Marc Brunel devised a cutting shield that could protect workers as they dug under the river and became the principal that is still

The Brunel Museum

The Brunel Museum is housed in what was the steam-driven pumping station *(left)* for the Thames Tunnel. It is a celebration of the life and work of Marc and Isambard Kingdom Brunel.

Surrey Water

The Thames Tunnel, 1843

Rotherhithe Overground

used in tunnelling today. Brunel's son, Isambard Kingdom Brunel, became the resident engineer at the age of nineteen. The tunnel

Brunel Road

Rotherhithe Tunnel

was beset with major problems, including toxic gases (the Thames was still a sewer at this point) and sudden flooding, both of which caused the project to come close to bankruptcy in 1828. The venture was saved and completed by a Parliamentary loan. This being the first ever construction of a tunnel under a river it attracted interest from all over the world. Visitors would pay to view the work in progress, despite the risk of flooding and gas. In 1843, the tunnel finally opened to pedestrian traffic, each paying one penny per visit. Despite its initial success, the tunnel never became a passageway for horse-drawn traffic. The tunnel was sold and re-opened in 1869 as part of the East London Railway. Today it forms part of the London Overground network.

Surrey Commercial Docks

The Rotherhithe peninsula was once totally dominated by the Surrey Commercial Docks – a set of ten interconnected inland harbours that took their names from the areas of the globe that they traded with (Russia, Quebec, Norway, etc). Over 80 per cent (186 hectares) of the peninsula was dug to create this network of inland docks and warehousing. It became hugely successful during the nineteenth century. However, during the Second World War many of the docks and adjacent warehouses were damaged by bombing raids. The advent of containerisation in the 1960s led to larger ships unable to navigate the shallow reaches of the Thames and so the docks fell out of favour, finally closing in 1970. The entire area was included in the London Dockland Development Corporation's remit to redeploy land of the former docks into residential, retail and recreational usage.

As a consequence, all except two and a half of the docks were filled in and built over. Very little remains of the warehouses and wharves that lined the river and the docks. Much of the riverfront now consists of low-rise residential blocks.

ON THE OTHER BANK
Limehouse Marina lockgate
page 53

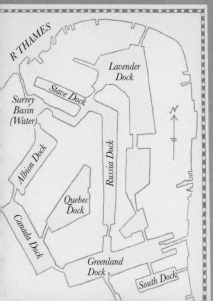

Left: The Surrey Commercial Docks c.1955.

Obelisk

This small stone obelisk at Pageant Crescent does not commemorate anything; it is purely decorative, and marks a focal point of a walk to the river from Salter Road

Grand Surrey Canal

This 'grand' canal never lived up to its name. Opening initially in 1807, with plans to reach Kingston in the west, it extended only as far as Camberwell. The barges that plied the canal carried mainly timber from the docks. Eventually the canal company placed its funds into the new, more profitable docks and the plans for canal expansion faded away. Much of the canal has been filled in following the docks' demise in the early 1970s.

Bascule Bridge

This bascule bridge *(below)* at the entrance to the Surrey Commercial Docks, was able to swing upwards to allow ships in and out. It is now no longer used as a bridge for motor vehicles, although pedestrians can still walk over it.

Left: The bascule bridge's location.

SURREY COMMERCIAL DOCKS

Surrey Water Bridge – Greenland Dock 3,295m

The Rotherhithe peninsula, once marshland, located between the City of London and the royal palace at Greenwich, became an ideal location for both commercial and naval dockyards. By 1800, a vast area had been converted into inland docks. Most of the warehouses and docks have gone and have been replaced with housing.

Nelson Dock

Rotherhithe Street

SURREY DOCKS FARM

Surrey Docks Farm

This working farm was established in 1975 on former dockland space. The land was previously used as a timber wharf and later the site of the river ambulance and fire services. The urban farm keeps numerous types of domestic farm animals, includes a horticulture section and is an educational resource for local schools and the community.

Surrey Docks Farm

Greenland Dock

In 1696 an Act of Parliament established the creation of London's first inland dock. At 4 hectares in size, it could hold 120 merchant ships within sheltered moorings for repairs and refitting. Originally known as Howland Great Wet Dock, it opened in 1700. By the 1720s, Greenland whaling ships began to dock here to process the blubber into oil and offload related produce. Consequently the dock was renamed Greenland Dock. Within a century and with the decline of whale imports, the dock was importing timber and grain. By the later nineteenth century it became a point of departure and arrival for passenger liners. This is the largest and oldest survivor of all the Surrey Commercial Docks. It is now a marina and watersports centre.

Odessa Street

Greenland Pier

Greenland Dock

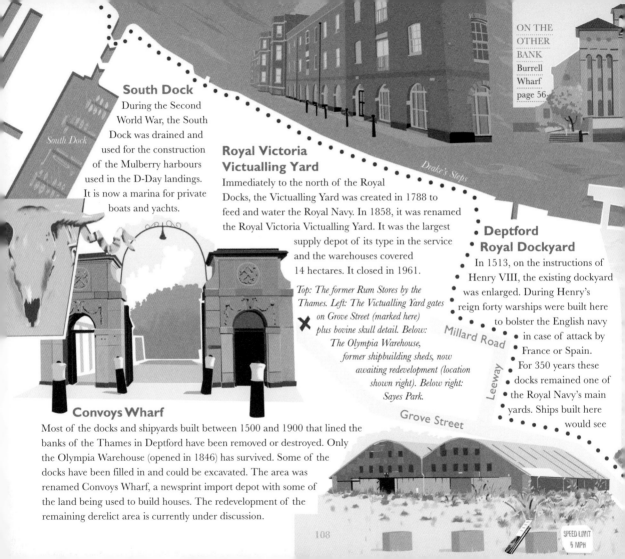

ON THE OTHER BANK
Burrell Wharf page 56.

South Dock

During the Second World War, the South Dock was drained and used for the construction of the Mulberry harbours used in the D-Day landings. It is now a marina for private boats and yachts.

Royal Victoria Victualling Yard

Immediately to the north of the Royal Docks, the Victualling Yard was created in 1788 to feed and water the Royal Navy. In 1858, it was renamed the Royal Victoria Victualling Yard. It was the largest supply depot of its type in the service and the warehouses covered 14 hectares. It closed in 1961.

Top: The former Rum Stores by the Thames. Left: The Victualling Yard gates on Grove Street (marked here) plus bovine skull detail. Below: The Olympia Warehouse, former shipbuilding sheds, now awaiting redevelopment (location shown right). Below right: Sayes Park.

Deptford Royal Dockyard

In 1513, on the instructions of Henry VIII, the existing dockyard was enlarged. During Henry's reign forty warships were built here to bolster the English navy in case of attack by France or Spain. For 350 years these docks remained one of the Royal Navy's main yards. Ships built here would see

Convoys Wharf

Most of the docks and shipyards built between 1500 and 1900 that lined the banks of the Thames in Deptford have been removed or destroyed. Only the Olympia Warehouse (opened in 1846) has survived. Some of the docks have been filled in and could be excavated. The area was renamed Convoys Wharf, a newsprint import depot with some of the land being used to build houses. The redevelopment of the remaining derelict area is currently under discussion.

108

SPEED LIMIT 5 MPH

DEPTFORD

Greenland Dock – Deptford Creek 3,110m

Along this stretch of riverside, now adorned with residential housing and wasteland, was once a great powerhouse of Royal Navy shipbuilding. Very little remains of 500 years of maritime history.

Former Deptford Power Station pier

Memorial to Tsar Peter the Great

Deptford Creek

The restored and converted Payne's Paper Wharf

Former Foreign Cattle Market Pier

Watergate Street

Prince Street

Evelyn Street

action against the Spanish Armada in 1588 and at the Battle of Trafalgar in 1805. Its royal associations became further embedded when in 1581 Queen Elizabeth I knighted Frances Drake on the *Golden Hinde*, moored by what is now known as Drake's Steps, on his return from circumnavigating the globe. Tsar Peter the Great lived at Sayes Court in 1698 in a house belonging to writer and diarist John Evelyn. The Tsar worked incognito in the dockyards to learn about shipbuilding. James Cook's HMS *Endeavour* was refitted here in 1768, prior to his voyage to 'discover' Australia and New Zealand. The dockyard's location would ultimately be its downfall, as larger vessels could not reach the shallower waters of the Thames. The Royal Naval docks at Portsmouth and Chatham, with deeper channels, were able to build and service these ships.

The Royal Docks closed in 1869 and became the Foreign Cattle Market. Prior to refrigeration, animals had to be kept alive during transit. The cattle were slaughtered on the quayside and processed before being moved on to market.

Deptford Power Station

The world's first large-scale electrical power generating station, created by Sebastian de Ferranti, was built on this site in 1889. It produced high-voltage alternating current, the system universally in use today. Like other power stations on the river it had access to supplies of coal by ship and water for cooling. It ceased generating in 1983.

Deptford Creek

This creek forms the mouth of the River Ravensbourne and is the site of Roman and Saxon settlements. A series of food mills, factories and a gin distillery used to line its banks.

The former Deptford Power Station. It was demolished in 1992.

109

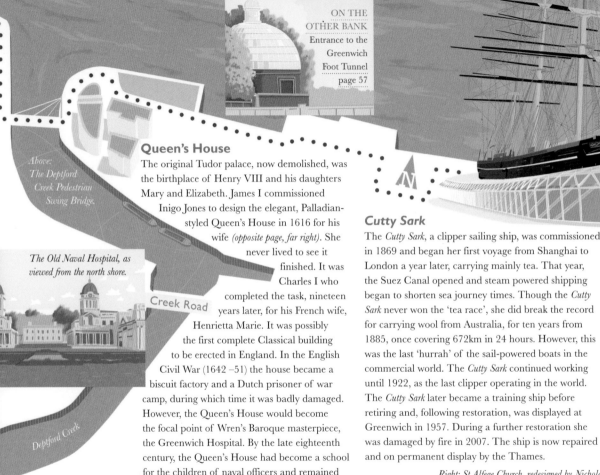

ON THE
OTHER BANK
Entrance to the
Greenwich
Foot Tunnel
page 57

*Above:
The Deptford
Creek Pedestrian
Swing Bridge.*

*The Old Naval Hospital, as
viewed from the north shore.*

Creek Road

Deptford Creek

Queen's House

The original Tudor palace, now demolished, was
the birthplace of Henry VIII and his daughters
Mary and Elizabeth. James I commissioned
Inigo Jones to design the elegant, Palladian-
styled Queen's House in 1616 for his
wife *(opposite page, far right)*. She
never lived to see it
finished. It was
Charles I who
completed the task, nineteen
years later, for his French wife,
Henrietta Marie. It was possibly
the first complete Classical building
to be erected in England. In the English
Civil War (1642 –51) the house became a
biscuit factory and a Dutch prisoner of war
camp, during which time it was badly damaged.
However, the Queen's House would become
the focal point of Wren's Baroque masterpiece,
the Greenwich Hospital. By the late eighteenth
century, the Queen's House had become a school
for the children of naval officers and remained
so until 1933. Today it is part of the National
Maritime Museum.

Cutty Sark

The *Cutty Sark*, a clipper sailing ship, was commissioned
in 1869 and began her first voyage from Shanghai to
London a year later, carrying mainly tea. That year,
the Suez Canal opened and steam powered shipping
began to shorten sea journey times. Though the *Cutty
Sark* never won the 'tea race', she did break the record
for carrying wool from Australia, for ten years from
1885, once covering 672km in 24 hours. However, this
was the last 'hurrah' of the sail-powered boats in the
commercial world. The *Cutty Sark* continued working
until 1922, as the last clipper operating in the world.
The *Cutty Sark* later became a training ship before
retiring and, following restoration, was displayed at
Greenwich in 1957. During a further restoration she
was damaged by fire in 2007. The ship is now repaired
and on permanent display by the Thames.

*Right: St Alfege Church, redesigned by Nicholas
Hawksmoor and consecrated in 1718. On this spot in
1012, St Alfege was beaten to death by Danish raiders.*

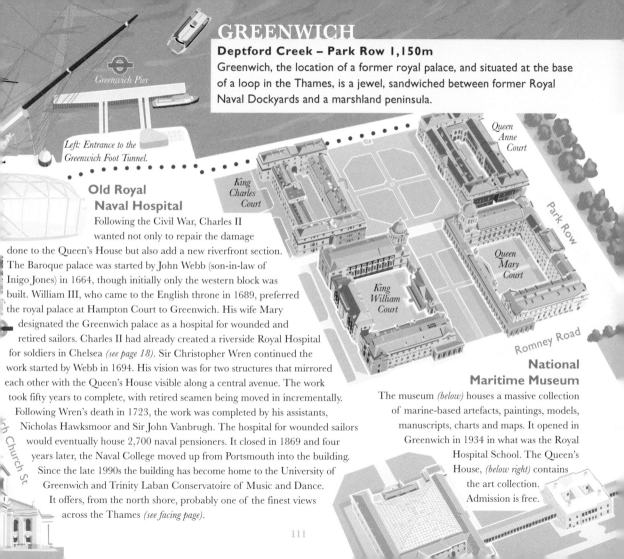

GREENWICH

Deptford Creek – Park Row 1,150m

Greenwich, the location of a former royal palace, and situated at the base of a loop in the Thames, is a jewel, sandwiched between former Royal Naval Dockyards and a marshland peninsula.

Greenwich Pier

Left: Entrance to the Greenwich Foot Tunnel.

Queen Anne Court

King Charles Court

Queen Mary Court

King William Court

Park Row

Romney Road

Old Royal Naval Hospital

Following the Civil War, Charles II wanted not only to repair the damage done to the Queen's House but also add a new riverfront section. The Baroque palace was started by John Webb (son-in-law of Inigo Jones) in 1664, though initially only the western block was built. William III, who came to the English throne in 1689, preferred the royal palace at Hampton Court to Greenwich. His wife Mary designated the Greenwich palace as a hospital for wounded and retired sailors. Charles II had already created a riverside Royal Hospital for soldiers in Chelsea *(see page 18)*. Sir Christopher Wren continued the work started by Webb in 1694. His vision was for two structures that mirrored each other with the Queen's House visible along a central avenue. The work took fifty years to complete, with retired seamen being moved in incrementally. Following Wren's death in 1723, the work was completed by his assistants, Nicholas Hawksmoor and Sir John Vanbrugh. The hospital for wounded sailors would eventually house 2,700 naval pensioners. It closed in 1869 and four years later, the Naval College moved up from Portsmouth into the building. Since the late 1990s the building has become home to the University of Greenwich and Trinity Laban Conservatoire of Music and Dance. It offers, from the north shore, probably one of the finest views across the Thames *(see facing page)*.

National Maritime Museum

The museum *(below)* houses a massive collection of marine-based artefacts, paintings, models, manuscripts, charts and maps. It opened in Greenwich in 1934 in what was the Royal Hospital School. The Queen's House, *(below right)* contains the art collection. Admission is free.

Church St

GREENWICH PENINSULA

Park Row – O₂ Arena 3,085m

On this former marshy peninsula no inland docks were ever built, nor did the full industrialised sprawl of Bermondsey, Rotherhithe and Deptford ever fully develop. Consequently very few people lived here until the twenty-first century. The arrival of the Millennium Dome in 2000 has improved the profile of the peninsula immensely.

The Trafalgar Tavern

This Regency-style public house *(right)* was opened in 1837 and became the haunt of many Victorian writers, including Wilkie Collins and Charles Dickens (it features in *Our Mutual Friend*, 1865). Politicians would travel down from Westminster by barge to partake of the famous whitebait suppers. The pub was damaged during the Second World War, but was restored and reopened in 1965.

Park Row

Crane St

Trafalgar Tavern

Trinity Hospital

0° longitude

Greenwich Power Station

Ballast Quay

Harbour Master's Office

Above: The Trafalgar Tavern. Below: The Harbour Master's Office.

Greenwich Power Station

This is a back-up electricity power station used by the London Underground network in cases of emergency *(left)*. Though now powered by gas and oil, it was, when commissioned in 1902, a coal-fired station receiving its raw material by colliers. The four stumpy chimneys have been truncated to two thirds of their original height.

Trinity Hospital

Struggling under the shadows of the neighbouring power station is a delicate Gothic almshouse, Trinity Hospital *(left)*. Founded in 1613, by the Earl of Northampton, but rebuilt, as it currently appears, in 1812.

112

ON THE OTHER BANK

Entrance to
West India
Dock
page 59

0° Longitude: Prime Meridian

The International Meridian Conference, held in Washington DC in 1884, agreed that the arbitrary meridian line would pass through Greenwich, East London. The Royal Greenwich Observatory was the location where longitude research had been calculated. This line had already been defined in the *Nautical Almanac*, first published in 1767, and had already been accepted by a large proportion of navigators. The prime meridian divides the globe into east and west.

0° longitude

A Slice of Reality

Standing on the foreshore of the Thames, close to the 0₂ Arena, sits this vertical slice of a ship *(right)*. It was created by the sculptor Richard Wilson.

*Below: The 0₂ Arena.
Bottom: Northbound gate of the Blackwall Tunnel.*

Blackwall Tunnel

Towards the end of the nineteenth century, despite the increasing number of new bridges over the Thames, the demand for more crossings grew, especially to the east of London and around the new docks. A bridge over the river at this point would have been too expensive as it would have to be high enough to allow masted ships to pass freely underneath. The first tunnel had been proposed by Sir Joseph Bazalgette, at the request of the Metropolitan Board of Works, in 1880s. Under the control of the newly formed London County Council in 1889, Sir Alexander Binnie was appointed to design a single-bore tunnel to form a link between Blackwall and the Greenwich Peninsula. It opened in 1897. However, by the 1930s, the flow of motor vehicles was already outgrowing its capacity. It was not until the 1960s that work started on the new eastern tunnel, which finally opened in 1967.

Blackwall Tunnel Approach

*North Greenwich
Underground*

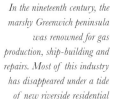

In the nineteenth century, the marshy Greenwich peninsula was renowned for gas production, ship-building and repairs. Most of this industry has disappeared under a tide of new riverside residential dwellings.

Emirates Air Line

Opening in 2012 in time for the Olympics, and at a cost of £60 million, this 1,100m long cable car links North Greenwich to the Royal Docks.

North Greenwich Pier

Left & below: The O₂ Arena

North Greenwich Underground

The Emirates Air Line cable car station

Quantum Cloud

This 30m high sculpture *(left)* was created by Antony Gormley in 1999, as part of the Millennium Dome project. Within the grid of steel, a human figure can be seen.

Greenwich Peninsula Ecology Park

This is an 11 hectare freshwater habitat with water pumped up from a borehole into a man-made lake. The ecology park was salvaged from former polluted industrial land. Now, as marshland, it reflects the original status of the peninsula. It is home to much diverse wildlife.

The O₂ Arena

Formerly known as the Millennium Dome, this structure was designed by Lord Richard Rogers as an exhibition space to celebrate the millennium. It opened on the evening of 31 December 1999 and was located here because of its proximity to the prime meridian. The Dome forms the largest single-roofed structure in the world and covers 93,000m². Following the closure of the exhibition at the end of 2000 it was converted into a large music and entertainment venue with a capacity of 20,000.

Greenwich Yacht Club

Greenwich Peninsula Ecology Park

BUGSBY'S REACH

O₂ Arena – Thames Barrier Visitor Centre 3,450m

The last stretch of this London Thames Path walk encompasses an eclectic combination of an ecology park, an ancient marine aggregate dock, a vast entertainment venue and a tidal control barrier.

The Thames Barrier

The barriers are located on the bed of the river, between the visible chrome fins. When rotated upright the barriers are 20m high. At times of flood risk, such as spring tides or tidal surges, the barriers are rotated into position. This operation takes a total of 90 minutes. This creates an 'empty pool' upstream, into which the excess rain water can run into without being held up by the incoming tide. It is believed that by 2030 the barrier may become gradually ineffective in holding back the rising sea levels and a replacement will be required.

Marine Aggregates Dock

The Angerstein and Murphy wharves form a 13 hectare plot for the import and grading of marine-dredged construction aggregates. Every year, 2.5 million tonnes of aggregates are brought in by ship, making these wharves the largest sea-dredged terminal in Europe. The finished aggregates, leaving by train and truck, are used largely in the UK construction industry. Aggregates have been imported here for nearly 200 years.

Angerstein & Murphy's Wharves

*Below: The Thames Barrier Control Centre
Right: The Information Centre & café.*

Unity Way

How the Barrier Works

1. The barrier sits on the river bed, allowing the Thames to flow normally and river traffic to pass through freely.

2. In the event of a tidal surge or a spring tide, the barrier is raised (as shown here) to hold the sea water back. The river water flowing down the Thames (from London) is allowed to build up against the barrier until the tide subsides and the barrier lowered.

◁ London

Sea ▷

Riverside

THE LONDON THAMES
CROSSINGS

A map of all the bridges and tunnels across and under the River
Thames, including the dates they were opened, from Putney to the
Blackwall Tunnel, plus the principal architects involved.

Left: Waterloo Bridge. Below right: Entrance
to the Blackwall Tunnel. Opposite page:
Lambeth Bridge.

Westminster Bridge
1750 Charles Labelye
1862 Thomas Page and Charles Barry

Lambeth Bridge
1862 Peter William Barlow
1932 George Humphreys

Chelsea Bridge
1858 Thomas Page
1937 G. Topham Forrest and
E.P. Wheeler

Battersea Bridge
1772 Henry Holland
1890 Sir Joseph Bazalgette

Wandsworth Bridge
1873 Julian Tolmé
1940 Sir Thomas
Peirson Frank

Vauxhall Bridge
1816 James Walker
1906 Sir Alexander
Binnie and Maurice
Fitzmaurice

Putney Bridge
1729 Sir Joseph Ackworth
1886 Sir Joseph Bazalgette

**Grosvenor Railway
Bridge**
1860 John Fowler
1866 Charles Fox
(additional bridge)

Putney Railway Bridge
1889 William Jacomb

Albert Bridge
1873 Rowland Mason Ordish

Battersea Railway Bridge
1863 William Baker and
T.H. Bertram

N

W

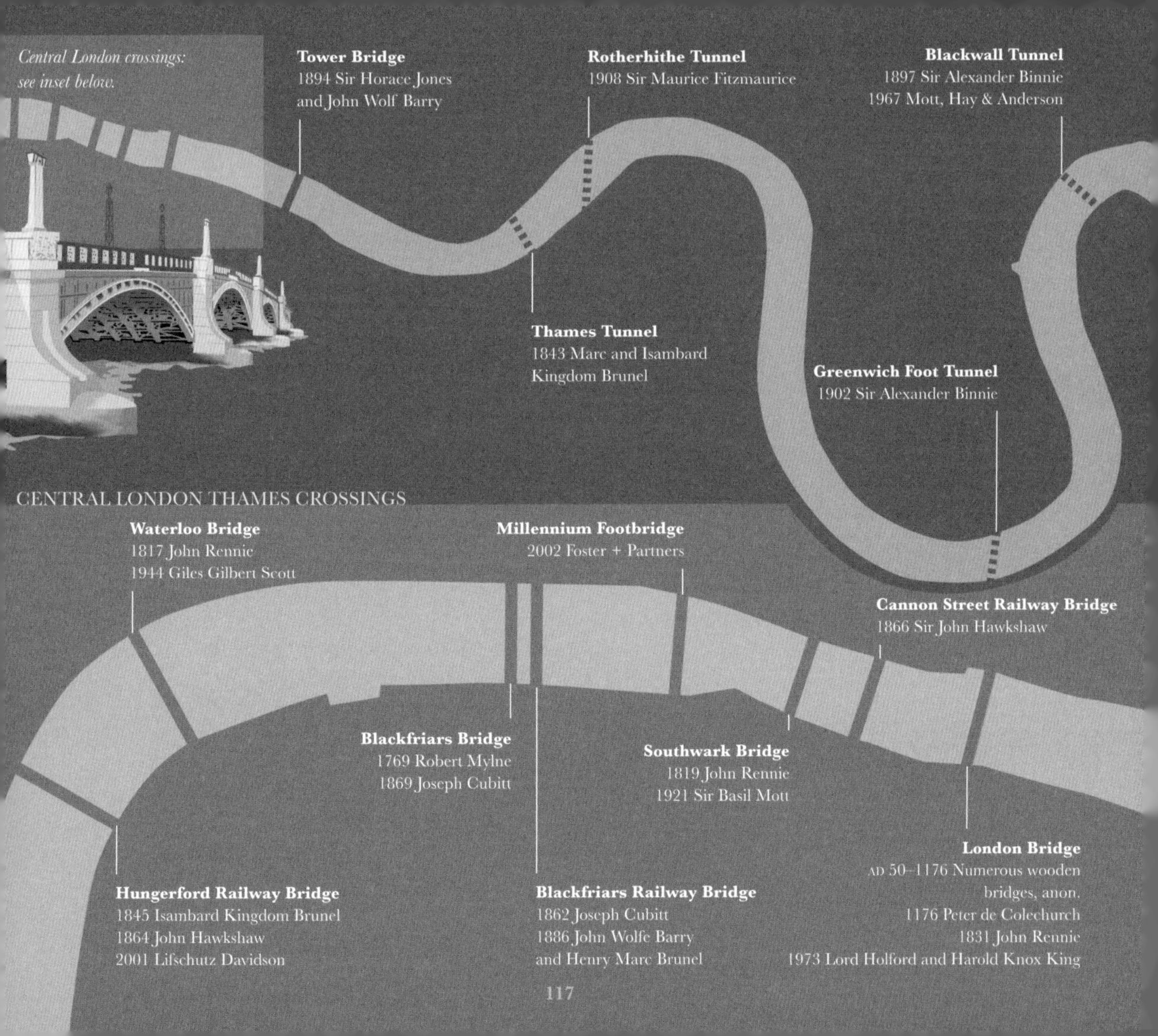

Central London crossings:
see inset below.

Tower Bridge
1894 Sir Horace Jones
and John Wolf Barry

Rotherhithe Tunnel
1908 Sir Maurice Fitzmaurice

Blackwall Tunnel
1897 Sir Alexander Binnie
1967 Mott, Hay & Anderson

Thames Tunnel
1843 Marc and Isambard
Kingdom Brunel

Greenwich Foot Tunnel
1902 Sir Alexander Binnie

CENTRAL LONDON THAMES CROSSINGS

Waterloo Bridge
1817 John Rennie
1944 Giles Gilbert Scott

Millennium Footbridge
2002 Foster + Partners

Cannon Street Railway Bridge
1866 Sir John Hawkshaw

Blackfriars Bridge
1769 Robert Mylne
1869 Joseph Cubitt

Southwark Bridge
1819 John Rennie
1921 Sir Basil Mott

London Bridge
AD 50–1176 Numerous wooden
bridges, anon.
1176 Peter de Colechurch
1831 John Rennie
1973 Lord Holford and Harold Knox King

Hungerford Railway Bridge
1845 Isambard Kingdom Brunel
1864 John Hawkshaw
2001 Lifschutz Davidson

Blackfriars Railway Bridge
1862 Joseph Cubitt
1886 John Wolfe Barry
and Henry Marc Brunel

London City Airport

The airport was constructed as a part of the London Dockland Development with the main runway and terminal being built adjacent to the Royal Albert Dock. The first commercial flight landed in October 1987. Because of the short runway, only smaller aircraft can access the airport. Destinations are mainly to the UK and Europe.

Rainham Marshes

These ancient marshes must be similar to those that lined the Thames, around London 2,000 years ago. The nature reserve, once a firing range for the Ministry of Defence, is now run by the RSPB. It is home to a wide range of birds, wetland plants and insects.

Above: The Port of Tilbury. Below: The RSPB Environment & Education Centre, Rainham Marshes.

Port of Tilbury

Throughout the later part of the nineteenth century the docks of London became increasingly unable to accommodate the ever larger ships. Their draughts were too deep for the relatively shallow Thames. A new port was sited and opened at Tilbury in 1886. The Dock was, in the late 1960s, adapted to handle containerisation. It was no coincidence that the London Docks went into steep decline in the 1970s.

Crossness

Rainham Marshes

RSPB

M25

The Thames Barrier

Ferry

Woolwich Ferry

There has been a ferry *(above)* operating at this location on the Thames for over 500 years. During the nineteenth century, the link became vital for workers and suppliers, following the creation of the Royal Arsenal at Woolwich and the Royal Docks. Since 1880s the service has been free to both vehicles and foot passengers.

The Queen Elizabeth II Bridge

The bridge, better known as the Dartford Crossing *(right)*, is part of the link across and under the Thames that includes two tunnels and connects to the M25. Demands on the tunnels became so huge, following the opening of the motorway that frequent congestion and delays occurred. A 450m wide 'cable-stayed' bridge was built using private finance and opened in 1991.

Dartford

Eurostar A broken tunnel under the Thames

Port of Tilbury

THE THAMES ESTUARY

Tilbury Fort

The original structure was a Tudor fort established by Henry VIII in 1539 to protect London against potential naval attacks by the Dutch and the Spanish. The defences were remodelled, on the instructions of Charles II, into the angular ramparts visible today. During the First World War, a Zeppelin

Tilbury Fort

airship was shot down by anti-aircraft guns sited within the grounds. It is no longer a military establishment and the fort is operated by English Heritage.

Tilbury Fort

Thames Haven

Until 1999, this was an oil refinery site established by Shell Oil in 1916. It is now a deepwater shipping port.

Canvey Island

Coalhouse Fort

The Crowstone

The obelisk on the shore at Westcliff, Essex, along with a similar marker at Yantlet Creek on the Kentish shore, defines the eastern most boundary of the Port of London Authority's power. The stone is located some 54km from London Bridge.

Westcliff-on-Sea

North Kent Marshes

Isle of Grain

North Kent Marshes

A complex of ancient coastal marshland that covers over 13,000 hectares from Gravesend to Whitstable, much of which has been enclosed by a medieval sea wall.

Coalhouse Fort

A defensive blockhouse was created at Coalhouse by Henry VIII in 1540 and was part of a network of forts to protect London. The Victorians rebuilt the artillery battery, which opened in 1874 (*left*), and was designed to work in conjunction with forts on the Kent shore to hit enemy shipping with a triangle of fire. Despite many upgrades, the guns never saw action against enemy shipping.

ACKNOWLEDGEMENTS

In walking and researching the London Thames Path, I've met numerous people who've assisted me in creating this book. My thanks to the following: Marion Watson and Judy Bracewell, church watchers at St James Garlickhythe ❧ The Revd Philip Warner of St Magnus the Martyr ❧ Ken Titmus (the Old Map Man) for his excellent guided tours of Pimlico and Vauxhall ❧ Teresa Lundquist (and Nick Lacey) for her time to show me around the fabulous Tower Bridge Moorings (at Downings Roads) ❧ Adrian Evans, Thames Festival director ❧ Christine Adam for her legal explanation of rights of way in relation to properties adjoining tidal rivers ❧ Gillian Allison and her fellow tour guides at Lambeth Palace ❧ Malcolm Crayton for further enlightenment regarding the mysteries of the 'Wren' plaque at 49 Bankside (in addition to the wonderful *The House on the Thames* by Gillian Tindall) ❧ Stephen Potter of the Southwark Local History Library and Archives ❧ Clare Wincza of the SS Robin Trust ❧ Paul Kellaway and his blog on the Wapping Project ❧ Andy Merriman for his valuable comments and feedback on *A Word on the Water* pages ❧ The web-based maps of Open Street, Bing, Apple and Google ❧ My agent, Sheila Ableman ❧ Andrew Dunn and Michael Brunstrom of Frances Lincoln for giving me (almost) free reign in the appearance and control of this book ❧ And finally thanks to my wife, Sheila Fathers, for proofing my sometimes dubious copy.

BIBLIOGRAPHY

Author(s)	Title	Publisher	Year
Ackroyd, Peter	Thames: Sacred River	Vintage	2008
Atterbury, Paul	The Doulton Story	Victor	1979
Bacon, George W. & Hyde, Ralph	The A to Z of Victorian London	Harry Margary	1987
Bead, Geoffrey	The Work of Christopher Wren	Bloomsbury Books	1987
Bolton, Tom	London's Lost Rivers	Strange Attractor Press	2011
Bradley, Simon & Pevsner, Nikolaus	London 1: The City of London	Penguin	1999
Bradley, Simon & Pevsner, Nikolaus	London 6: Westminster	Yale University Press	2005
Cherry, Bridget & Pevsner, Nikolaus	London 2: South	Yale University Press	2002
Cherry, Bridget & Pevsner, Nikolaus	London 3: North West	Penguin	1999
Cherry, Bridget, O'Brien, Charles & Pevsner, Nikolaus	London 5: East	Yale University Press	2005
Craig, Charles, Diprose, Graham & Seaborne, Mike	London's Changing Riverscape	Frances Lincoln	2009
Clapham, Phoebe	Thames Path in London	Aurum Press	2012
Croad, Stephen	Liquid History: The Thames Through Time	Batsford	2003
Downes, Kerry	Sir Christopher Wren: The Design of St Paul's Cathedral	The AIA Press	1990
Elborough, Travis & Rennison, Nick	A London Year	Frances Lincoln	2013
Fathers, David	The Regent's Canal	Frances Lincoln	2012
Howard, Rachel & Nash, Bill	Secret London: An Unusual Guide	Jonglez	2011
Hampson, Tim	London's Riverside Pubs	New Holland	2011
Jones, Sydney R.	Thames Triumphant	Studio	1943
Matthews, Peter	London's Bridges	Shire	2008
Starkey, David	Royal River	Royal Museum Greenwich	2012
Talling, Paul	London's Lost Rivers	Random House Books	2011
Tindall, Gillian	The House by the Thames	Pimlico	2007
Winn, Christopher	I Never Knew That About The Thames	Ebury Press	2010
	Reference Atlas of Greater London	John Bartholomew & Sons	1961
	The Brunels' Tunnel	The Brunel Museum	2006
	Dome	Booth Clibborn Editions	2000
	The Shard. The Official Guide Book	Thames & Hudson	2013
	Westminster Abbey Guide	Westminster Abbey	2013

INDEX

O₂ Arena 59, 113, 114
49 Bankside 91

Ackroyd, Peter 53
A Clerk's Tale (Chaucer) 50
Aethelred, King 37
Albert Bridge 70, 116
Albert Embankment, The 31, 76, 79
Albion Riverside 69
Alfred, King 37
All Saints, Fulham 12, 66
Angerstein & Murphy's Wharves 115
Archbishops of Canterbury
  Archbishop Baldwin 78
  Archbishop Cranmer 78
Arnold, Benedict 69
Ashmolean Museum 78
Ashmole, Elias 78
Austen, Jane 26

Baines, Sir Frank 23
Banco Ambrosiano 103
Bankside 23, 72
Banqueting Hall 28
Barlow, Peter William 77
Barry, Sir Charles 24, 28, 116
bascule Bridge 106
Batrichsey 65
Battersea 65
Battersea Bridge 16, 31, 116
Battersea Creek 68
Battersea Dogs & Cats Home 72
Battersea Fun Fair 71
Battersea Park 20, 70
Battersea Power Station 21, 72
Battersea Railway Bridge 116

Battle of Britain memorial 28
Bazalgette, Sir Joseph 16, 20, 29, 30, 59, 66, 75, 102, 113, 116
Belfast 97
Belloc, Hilaire 17
Belvedere Tower, The 15
Bentham, Jeremy 22
Beormund Eye 65
Bermondsey 57, 65, 100
Betjeman, John 26
Big Ben 24, 25
Binnie, Sir Alexander 57, 74, 113, 116, 117
Bishop Henry of Blois 93
Bishop Stopford 12
Bishop of Winchester 92
Blackfriars Bridge 35, 38, 39, 65, 95, 102, 117
Blackfriars Railway Bridge 46, 90, 117
Black Friar, The 36
Blackwall 60
Blackwall Tunnel 31, 57, 113, 117
Blake, William 26, 50, 68, 69, 79
Bligh, Captain 78
Blitz, The 59
Bloodworth, Sir Thomas 42
Boat Race, The 12
Boleyn, Anne 45
Borough Market 92
Boucher, Catherine 69
Boudica 28, 29
Bowbelle 103
Bow Creek 60, 61
Bow Creek Ecology Park 61
Bridewell Palace 35
Bridge House Estate 95
British Film Institute, The 86
Brompton and Piccadilly Circus Railway 15
Brontë sisters 26

Bronze Age Pier 74
Browning, Robert 26
Brunel, Henry Marc 46, 117
Brunel, Isambard Kingdom 17, 32, 56, 105, 117
Brunel, Marc Isambard 17, 105
Brunel Museum 105
Burghers of Calais, The 24
Burke, Thomas 53
Burns, John 68
Burrell Wharf 56
Butler's Wharf 100
Buxton, Charles 24
Buxton, Thomas 24

Cadogan, Dr William 13
Calvi, Roberto 35, 103
Canada Square 54
Canary Wharf 54
Canary Wharf Pier 54
Cannon Street Railway Bridge 117
Cannon Street station 39
Canterbury Tales, The 50
Captain Kidd 48
Cardinal John Morton 78
Carlyle Mansion 17
Carlyle, Thomas 17
Caro, Sir Anthony 91
Catherine of Aragon 36
Caunt, Benjamin 25
César Pelli & Associates 54
Chambers, William 34
Charing Cross station 32
Charles I 28, 110
Charles II 18, 111
Chatham, London and Dover Railway 90
Chaucer, Geoffrey 26
Chelsea Bridge 20, 116
Chelsea College of Art 22
Chelsea Creek 15

Chelsea Embankment 16, 18, 31
Chelsea Flower Show 19
Chelsea Harbour 14, 15
Chelsea Harbour Pier 15
Chelsea Manor 17
Chelsea Old Church (All Saints) 17
Chelsea Pensioners 18
Chelsea Physic Garden 18
Chelsea Waterworks Company 20
Cherry Gardens Pier 101
Cheyne Walk 16, 17, 69
cholera 30
Churchill, Sir Winston 36
City Canal 59
City Hall 97
Coade stone 48, 82
Clapham Junction 68
Cleopatra's Needle 33
Clink Museum, The 92
Clore Gallery 23
Coalhouse Fort 119
Coin Street Community Builders 87
Coleridge, Samuel Taylor 26
Collins, Wilkie 112
Colquhoun, Patrick 48
Conan Doyle, Arthur 50, 52
Conrad, Sir Terence 100
Convoys Wharf 108
Cornhill 38
Corporation of London 38
Counter's Creek 15
County Hall 82
Courtauld Institute of Art 34
Covent Garden 73
Craven Cottage 19
Cremorne Pleasure Gardens 15, 16
Cringle Dock Transfer Station 72
Cromwell, Oliver 26, 34, 66, 76
Cromwell, Thomas 45
Crosby Hall 16

Crosby, John 16
Crowstone, The 119
Cubitt, Joseph 35, 117
Cubitt, William 58
Cubitt, Thomas 58, 70
Cubitt Town 58
Cubitt Wharf 57
Currey, Henry 79
Custom House 43, 50
Cutty Sark Gardens 57
Cutty Sark 110

Darwin, Charles 26
de Breaute, Sir Falkes 77
de Colechurch, Peter 94, 117
de Ferranti, Sebastian 109
Defensive Pillbox 13
Deptford Creek 109
Deptford Creek Pedestrian Swing
    Bridge 110
Deptford Power Station 109
Deptford Royal Dockyard 108
Design Museum, The 100
Dickens, Charles 26, 32, 49, 50, 53,
    76, 92, 95, 101, 102, 112
Ditchburn and Mare Shipbuilding
    Company 61
Dixon, Joseph 69
Docklands Light Railway 54, 60
Docklands Sailing and Watersports
    Centre 55
Doggett's Coat and Badge Race 81
Doggett, Thomas 81
Dolphin Square 21
D'Oyly Carte, Richard 33
Drake, Sir Frances 93, 109
Duke of Wellington 18, 24, 36
Eastern Dock 47
East India Company 60
East India Dock 60
East London Railway 105

Edgar, King 27
Edward the Confessor 24, 27
Edward I 45
Edward II 27
Edward III 25, 27, 59, 104
Edward V 27
Edward VIII 27
Effra, River 75
Ethelred, King 94
Eliot, George 17
Eliot, T.S. 17, 51
Elizabeth I 27, 109, 110
Elizabeth II 83
Elizabethan Schools, The 13
Endeavour, HMS 109
English Civil War 40, 66, 78, 110
Evelyn, John 88, 89, 109
ExCeL London, The 63
Execution Dock 48

Falcon Brook 68
Faraday, Michael 60
Farrell, Terry 32, 75
Farriner, Thomas 42
Fatboy's Diner 60
Fawkes, Guy 45
Festival of Britain 71, 83, 84
Fighting Temeraire, The 49, 104
Finer, Jem 61
Fishmongers' Hall 39
Fleet, River 35, 40
Fleming, Ian 17
Football Association 71
Fortress Wapping 47
Foster + Partners 69, 91, 97
Frost Fairs 88
Fulham FC 19
Fulham Palace 12
Fuller Clark, H. 36

Gabriel's Wharf 87
Gallion's Reach 103
Garden Museum, The 78
Gaskell, Elizabeth 17
George I 77
George V 52
Gilbert and Sullivan 33
Gilbert Scott, Sir Giles 72, 73, 85,
    90, 117
Globe Theatre, The 91
Golden Hinde 93, 109
Goodhart-Rendel, Harry Stuart 96
Gormley, Antony 114
Grand Surrey Canal 106
Grapes, The 53
Great Britain 56
Great Eastern, SS 55, 56
Greater London Authority 97
Greater London Council 82
Great Fire of London 36, 37, 40,
    41, 42, 43
Great Fire of Southwark, The 101
Greathead, James Henry 44
Great Western 56
Greaves, Walter 17
Greenland Dock 107
Greenland Pier 107
Greenwich Foot Tunnel 57, 111,
    117
Greenwich Hospital 110
Greenwich Peninsula 113
Greenwich Peninsula Ecology
    Park 114
Greenwich Power Station 112
Grey, Lady Jane 45
Grosvenor Canal 20
Grosvenor Railway Bridge 20, 116
Gun, The 59
Guy's Hospital 95, 99, 104
Guy, Thomas 99

Hall, Sir Benjamin 25
Hamilton, Lady Emma 59
Hammersmith Bridge 31
Hampstead Heath 35
Hampton Court 41, 111
Handel, George Fredric 26, 76, 77
Harbour Master's Office. 112
Hardy, Thomas 26
Harvard, John 93
Hawkshaw, Sir John 32, 39
Hawksmoor, Nicholas 27, 41,
    110, 111
Hay's Dock 97
Hay's Galleria 97
Hay's Wharf Company 96, 97
Henry I 37
Henry II 94
Henry III 24, 27, 33, 77, 95
Henry V 27
Henry VIII 17, 27, 28, 36, 45, 59,
    108, 110
Hepworth, Barbara 71
Hermitage Basin 47
Hermitage Moorings 47
Hermitage Riverside Memorial
    Gardens 46
Herzog & de Meuron 90
Hess, Rudolf 45
Hilton Dockland Riverside 107
Hitchcock, Alfred 102
Holborn Viaduct 35
Homer, Thomas 53
Hooke, Robert 41, 42
House of Commons 25
House of Lords 25
Houses of Parliament 24
Howard, Catherine 45
Howland Great Wet Dock 107
Hughes, Ted 26
Hungerford Bridge 32, 117
Hurlingham Club 13

Hurlingham Polo Association 13
Huskisson, William 21

Imperial Wharf 14
Imperial Wharf Overground 15
Inner Temple 34
Island Gardens 56
Isle of Dogs 47, 54, 56, 58, 59
Isle of Dogs Pumping Station 59

Jacob's Island 101
James, Henry 17
Jeffreys, George 49
Jerome, Jerome K. 51
'Jerusalem' 79
Jewel Tower 25
John, King 77
John Scott Russell shipyard 56
Jones, Christopher 104
Jones, Inigo 28, 110, 111
Jones, Sidney R. 53
Jones, Sir Horace 43, 46, 117
Jonson, Ben 26
Jubilee Gardens 83

K2, The 73
Keats, John 26
Kensington Canal 15
King Edward VII Memorial Park 52
King George V Docks 62
Kipling, Rudyard 5, 26
Knights Templar 34
Knott, Ralph 82
Kray Twins 45

Ladies Bridge 85
Lake Havasu, Arizona 96
Lambeth Bridge 77, 116
Lambeth Marsh 79
Lambeth Palace 78

Lasdun, Sir Denys 86
Lear, Edward 26
Lee Valley Park 60
Levellers, The 66
Liberty of the Clink, The 92
Liebig Extract of Meat Company 87
Lifschutz Davidson 32, 63, 117
Limehouse 52
Limehouse Basin 53
Limehouse Cut 59
Limehouse Golem 53
Limehouse Nights 53
Lion Brewery 82
London and Brighton Railway Company 32
London Bridge (see also Old London Bridge) 42, 43, 50, 88, 92, 96, 117
London City Airport 62, 118
London County Council 82
London Docklands Development Corporation 53, 54, 62, 106, 118
London Docks 47, 49, 70
London Dock Strike 58
London Eye, The 83
London Grain Elevator Company 63
London Heliport 68
London Hydraulic Power Company 44
London Overground 105
London Studios 86
London Weekend Television 86
Longplayer 61
Lots Road Power Station 15
Ludgate Hill 27, 38
Lyle Golden Syrup Tin 62

Maddox, Michael 77
Marchioness 103
Marine Aggregates Dock 115
Marine Police Force 48
Markov, Georgi 103
Marks Barfield 83
Marlowe, Christopher 26
Martin, John 30
Mary I 27
Masefield, John 51
Masthouse Terrace Pier 55
Matilda, Queen 37
Mayflower Pub, The 105
Mayflower 104
McColloch Oil Company, 96
McDougall Garden, Sir John 55
Metropolitan Board of Works 30, 70, 74, 113
MI5 23
MI6 75
Middle Temple 34
Millbank 22, 90
Millbank Estate 23
Millbank Penitentiary 22
Millbank Tower 23, 36
Millennium Bridge 95
Millennium Dome 114
Millennium Footbridge 91, 95, 117
Millennium Wheel 83
Milligan, Robert 54
Millwall Dock 55, 57
Millwall FC 57
Ministry of Defence, The 28
Monument, The 41, 42
Moore, Albert 87
Moore, Henry 24, 71
Moran, Christopher 16
More, Sir Thomas 16, 17, 45
Morton's Canning factory 57
Mozart, Wolfgang Amadeus 19
Mudchute Park and Farm 57

Museum of London Docklands 54
Music for the Royal Fireworks 76
Mylne, Robert 35

Narrow, The 53
Nash, John 53
National Maritime Museum 110, 111
Naval College 111
Neckinger, River 101
Nelson Dock 107
Nelson, Lord Horatio 33, 36, 59
New Covent Garden Flower Market 73
New Covent Garden Market 73
New Crane Stairs 48
New Model Army 66
New Spring Gardens 76
Newton, Issac 26
Nightingale, Florence 79
Nine Elms 73
Northern Low Level Sewer 29
North Kent Marshes 119

Olaf, King 94
Old Billingsgate Fish Market 43
Old London Bridge 80, 85, 94, 102
Old Royal Naval Hospital, The 111
Old Swan Pier 39, 81
Olympia Warehouse 108
Ordish, Rowland Mason 70, 116
Orwell, George 43
Our Mutual Friend 50, 51, 53
Outram, John 59
Owen Dobson, Frank 96
OXO Tower 87

Page, Thomas 20, 28
Palace of Westminster 79
Palace of Whitehall 24, 28
Pankhurst, Sylvia 17

Parry, Sir Hubert 79
Peace Pagoda, The 71
Peasants' Revolt 33
pedestrian ferry 107
Pennethorne, Sir James 70
Pepys, Samuel 49
Peter the Great 109
Piano, Renzo 99
Pimlico Gardens 21
Piranesi, Giovanni Battista 35
Poet's Corner 26
Pontoon Dock 63
Pool of London 43, 46
Portcullis House 28
Port of Tilbury 118
Price's Candle Factory 68
prime meridian 113
Princess Alice 103
Prospect of Whitby, The 49
Prothalamion 51
Pudding Lane 42
Pugin, Augustus W.N. 24, 25
Pump House Gallery 71
Purcell, Henry 26
Purcell Room 85
Putney Bridge 31, 66, 116
Putney Railway Bridge 12, 116
Putney Debates 66

Quantum Cloud 114
Queen Elizabeth Hall 85, 86
Queen Elizabeth II Bridge 118
Queenhithe 37
Queen Mary Steps 29
Queen's House 110

Rainham Marshes 118
Raleigh, Walter 50
Ranelagh Pleasure Gardens 19
Regent's Canal, The 22, 53
Rennie, John 38, 85, 95, 117

Ricci, Sebastiano 18
River Police Boatyard 48
Riverside and General Labourer's
    Union 58
Robertson, Sir Howard 83
Rodin, Auguste 24
Rogers, Lord Richard 114
Ronald Ward & Partners 23
Rossetti, Dante Gabriel 17
Rotherhithe Tunnel, The 52, 105,
    117
Royal Albert Dock 62, 118
Royal Courts of Justice 34
Royal Doulton 77
Royal Festival Hall 82, 84
Royal Greenwich Observatory 113
Royal Horticultural Society 19
Royal Hospital Chelsea 18, 111
Royal Mint 45
Royal National Lifeboat Institute
    103
Royal National Theatre 86
Royal Society 40
Royal Victoria Dock Bridge 63
Royal Victoria Docks 62
Royal Victoria Victualling Yard
    108

Sæbert, King 27
St Alfege 110
St Benet 41
St Clement Danes 41
St George's Square 21
St George Wharf 75
St James Garlickhythe 37, 41
St John's Old School 48
St Katherine Docks 21, 46, 47
St Magnus the Martyr 41, 42
St Margaret Lothbury 41
St Margaret Patten 41
St Margaret's 25

St Martin Ludgate 41
St Mary Abchurch 41
St Mary Battersea 69
St Mary Lambeth 77, 78
St Mary Overie 93
St Mary Overie Dock 93
St Mary Putney 66
St Mary the Virgin 104
St Michael Paternoster Royal 41
St Olaf House 96
St Paul's Cathedral 36, 41, 91
St Paul's Presbyterian Church 55
St Peter's Basilica 36
St Saviour 93
St Saviour's Dock 101
St Stephen's Walbrook 41
St Thomas à Becket 79
St Thomas' Hospital 79, 99
Saklatvala, Shapurji 68
Salter, Dr Alfred 104
Savoy Hotel 33
Savoy Palace 33
Scott, Sir Walter 26
Secret Intelligence Service HQ
    (MI6) 75
Sellar Property and LBQ Ltd 99
Seymour, Edward 34
Shad Thames 100
Shadwell Basin 47, 49
Shakespeare, Edmund 93
Shakespeare, William 26, 91, 93
Shard, The 99
Sheldon, Gilbert 40
Shell Centre, The 83
Shell Mex House 33
Silvertown 62
Skylon 84
Slice of Reality, A 113
Sloane, Sir Hans 17, 18
Smirke, Sir Robert 43
Smith, Sidney R.J. 23

Snow, Dr John 30
Soane, Sir John 73
Solid Waste Transfer Station 67
Somerset House 34
South Dock 108
Southwark 92
Southwark Bridge 38, 50, 95,
    103, 117
Southwark Cathedral 42, 93
Spenser, Edmund 51
Spiller's Millennium Mills 63
Spring Gardens 76
Stirling, Sir James 23
Stoker, Bram 21
Surrey Commercial Docks 49, 106
Surrey Docks Farm 107
Surrey Iron Railway 67

Tate Britain 22, 23
Tate Modern 23, 90
Tate, Sir Henry 23
Telford, Thomas 46
Temeraire, HMS 104
Temple 34
Temple, John 102
Tennyson, Alfred Lord 26
Thames Barrier Park 63
Thames Barrier, The 63, 115
Thames Haven 119
Thames House 23
Thames Ironworks and
    Shipbuilding Company 61
Thameslink 90
Thames Tunnel, The 105, 117
Thorney Island 24
Three Men in a Boat 51
Tilbury Fort 119
Tillett, Ben 58
Tobacco Dock 47
Tomb of the Unknown Warrior 27
Tono-Bungay 51

Tower Beach 44
Tower Bridge 31, 43, 46, 49, 52,
	95, 117
Tower Bridge Moorings 101
Tower of London, The 44
Tower Subway 44
Town of Ramsgate, The 47
Tradescant the Elder, John 78
Tradescant the Younger, John 77
Tradescant Trust 78
Trafalgar Tavern, The 112
Traitors' Gate 45
Trinity Buoy Wharf 60, 61
Trinity Hospital 112
Trinity House Workshop 60
Trinity Laban Conservatoire of
	Music and Dance 111
Turks Head, The 48
Turner, J.M.W. 16, 23, 49, 69, 104
Tuthmose III, Pharaoh 33
Tweed, John 17
Tyburn, River 22, 24
Tyler, Wat 39

Undercroft Skatepark, The 85
Unilever House 35
US Capitol 41
US Embassy 73
University of Greenwich 111

Vanbrugh, Sir John 41, 111
Vauxhall Bridge 57, 74, 116
Vauxhall Motors 77
Vauxhall Pleasure Gardens 74,
	76, 77
Vickers-Armstrong Group 23
Victoria, Queen 20, 28, 35, 70, 79
Victoria Embankment 29, 31, 34
Victoria Embankment Gardens
	32, 33
Victoria Park 70, 95

Victoria station 20
Victoria Tower 25
Vintners' Hall 37
Virginia Quay 60
Vokzal 77

Walbrook, River 11, 38, 94
Walbrook Wharf 38
Wanamaker, Sam 91
Wandle, River 67
Wandsworth Bridge 14, 67, 116
Wandsworth Park 66
Wapping 49
Wapping Hydraulic Power Station
	49
Wapping Old Stairs 80
Wapping Wall 49
Warrior 61
Waste Land, The 51
Waterloo Bridge 85, 86, 102, 117
watermen 80
Water Music 77
Webb, John 111
Wells, H.G. 51
Westbourne, River 19
Western Dock 47
Western Pumping Station 20
West Ham FC 61
West India Dock Company 59
West India Docks 54, 59
Westminster 24
Westminster Abbey 24, 27
Westminster Bridge 28, 116
Westminster Hall 25, 26, 34
Westminster Pier 28
West Mynstre 27
wherry boats 80
Whistler, James McNeill 16, 17
Whitehall Gardens 29
Wilberforce, William 24, 26
Wilde, Oscar 26

Wilford Associates 23
William I 44
William II 24
William III 111
William Walworth, Sir 39
Willoughby, Sir Hugh 52
Wilson, Richard 113
Wilson Steer, Philip 17
Winchester 93
Winchester Geese 92
Winchester Palace 93
Wolfe Barry, Sir John 39, 46, 117
Woodroffe, Edward 41
Woolwich Free Ferry 31, 118
Wordsworth, William 50
Worshipful Company of
	Fishmongers, The 39, 81
Worshipful Company of Watermen
	and Lightermen, The 81
Worshipful Society of Apothecaries,
	The 18
Wren, Sir Christopher 18, 28, 34,
	35, 36, 37, 40, 42, 43, 91, 110
Wycliffe, John 78

York House Watergate 32
Young's Ram Brewery 67

Zaha Hadid Architects 100

First published in 2015 by Frances Lincoln Ltd,
an imprint of The Quarto Group,
The Old Brewery, 6 Blundell Street,
London N7 9BH, United Kingdom
T (0)20 7700 6700 F (0)20 7700 8066
www.QuartoKnows.com

ISBN: 978-0-7112-3553-3

Printed and bound in China

6 8 9 7